Gumbo Bottoms Pure Pot Still Poets Society Presents:

A Drop of the Pure

Edited by Jon Freeland
and Jason Ryberg

OAC Press
Belle, Missouri

OAC
PRESS
OSAGE ARTS COMMUNITY

Copyright © Jason Ryberg, Jon Freeland, 2025
First Edition: 1 3 5 7 9 10 8 6 4 2
ISBN: 979-8-89975-014-4
LCCN: 2025938376

Logo created by: Patrick Hall

Acknowledgments:

The authors would like to thank the editors of the following publications where some of these poems (in one form or another) were formerly published:

Reported For Duty: Veteran's Anthology, 365 Days Poetry Anthology: Volume 3, The Gasconade Review Presents: Strange Days, Stranger Nights, The Roaring Junior Press Bestiary: Anthology of Monsters and Mythology, Wine Drunk Sidewalk: Ship Wrecked in Trumpland, Rye Whiskey Review, Oddball Magazine, Rusty Truck, Chewers Masticadores, Poetry Breakfast, Amethyst Review, Silver Birch Press, Ekphrastic Review, Spillwords, Paddler Press' volume Grace Notes, Cave Region Review, Live Nude Poems, Lothlorien Poetry Journal, Well-Versed 2021, As It Ought To Be Magazine, Pleiades, The Rumpus, Inside Columbia, Well Versed, Straywords, Okay Donkey, Gasconade Review, The Inflectionist Review, THRUSH, Journal of Compressed Creative Arts, Anti-Heroin Chic, MasticadoresUSA

Table of Contents:

Introduction:

Stephen Erangey, Owner Gumbo Bottoms Alehaus

A few years ago, pre-covid, I met Jon Freeland. It felt, at the time, like the many pleasant interactions I've had over thirty-odd years of being in the bar business. I tend to magnetically attach myself to creative people, regardless of the actual discipline.

Jon was one of those humans, and remains one of those humans. Again, I come from live music club bartending. I also come from the Republic of Ireland, Cork City to be specific, class of '87, Donnelly visa, 12 years old.

I grew up on punk rock, bards, storytellers, troubadours, actors, playwrights, musicians, singers, and of course poets. So a very natural, organic, common goal of simply reading poetry was an easy endeavor.

The day I met Jon, I immediately called my friend and mentor, Allen Tatman. Allen and I are brothers in mouth bullets, and tales of yore. I remember specifically reading a draft of a book Allen had written when I used to work for him and his lovely wife, Marilee, who is also a trusted mentor. I told him about my chat with Jon and...

BOOM!
Contact!
This feels good.

So once a month, on an otherwise lonely and sleepy Monday night in the fair city of Jefferson, in the great stateof Missouri, "Single Pot Still Poets Society" was birthed. What follows is our club's first attempt at a collective publication.

I love these people and I want to thank them for our "monthly sessions." Paddy Malone's Irish Pub & Gumbo Bottoms Alehaus proudly present Volume 1: A Drop of the Pure

Slainte,
Padrigh Stiofan

A Drop of the Pure

Gumbo Therapy

We gather each month in this house,
Friends drawn together by our words
And our love of words, and we
Listen and encourage and learn from
Those who come from so many
Places, to share our deepest loves,
And fears, and dreams.

For this man of words, some enlightened
And some oh, so silly, it is a time to
Find my center, to know I am at
Another home, to feel the warmth
Of those who know the power and
The solace of a well-turned phrase.

Each time I leave these walls, I am
Stronger, I am better, I am more
Comfortable in my own skin. So
I will listen with all my being, I will
Let each one know they are cherished,
And I will share my admiration
For their willingness to share a
Small part of themselves with me.

~ m. pottorff

Fuelogy

for Mark

Regard is a currency:
it can be saved and spent,
stolen, owed, and borrowed
for speculating futures.
It drives the highest powered
oil companies forward in black ink,
no way back in cold acquisition,
so fast that it misses
the chance to write
in the saltwater drips
(of a Son, Father, Teacher)
a child's challenge,
about roadside dogs
and ridiculous doctors.
The present of words
powers a person;
we are remembered
in remembering
and Regard is a currency,
infusing what was with
the power of now,
guarding themory
and pouring capital praise
because what is earned
may not be kept,
but what is Dad
will never die.

~ Jon Freeland

He slept in a one-room cabin

deep in the woods that night windows open wide to the
gospel of spring air which should have been glorious
beneath three blankets but the lock on the front door
had rusted out over time and he came to sleep uneasily
and it was no surprise when the nightmares arrived but
instead of a murderer or even a wayward meth addict
with a stolen crowbar crashing into the darkness with
a Nicholsonian grin anxiety produced an even more
terrible film a live shooter at the elementary school where
he worked the godawful drumbeats of gunshots the
alarm and the garbled instructions over the automated
intercom as he rushed twenty-two tiny panicked bodies
into a storage closet the size of a half bath only to
realize he'd forgotten the class roster though he counted
and counted he could not remember everyone's name
gagging on stomach acid trying gently to shush a crier
whose face he couldn't see once he turned out the lights
there were hands on his legs tiny hands grabbing at his
hands shuffling sounds in the corner and something
falling from a shelf he tried to tether himself to time
but could not keep from thinking of his youngest
daughter upstairs in the fourth grade room the ancient
door and wide window such slight barriers between her
and whatever desperately wanted to return them to the
Earth as dust fear with its ruthless intelligence playing
chess while everyone else was so busy always trying to
jump over top of their allies' checkers then morning the
heartpound the sweat the coffee and a question how
many others have this same dream behind doors locked
or unlocked in town or out in the woods each night in
the miraculous country of limitless Little Debbie snacks
the very first country in the world to put a human on
the moon

~ Justin Hamm

3

Jug Band Poet

A dozen poets gather
at Gumbo Bottoms Ale House
to celebrate the success of
a daylong poetry festival.
The place is packed, and everyone
is grooving to the jug band
music of The Diddy Wah Daddys.
It may not be poetry open mic night,
but Justin Hamm says what the hell
as the harmonica player steps aside
for a breather. He asks the band
if they're up for a little poetry
with their music. They're all in,
so, Justin steps up to the mic
and starts in with his poem.
Standup bass, banjos, clarinet,
and washboard join in, setting a beat
that Justin settles into, and the crowd
spends all their energy on applause,
grateful for *My Father's Money.*

~ Ken Gierke

Yes Sand

for Ken

It's a cruel trick of Greek
dichotomy, Elizabethan
alliteration, and the
need to pick a part
to create brand new -
straight from the fire,
the conflict could not
be on our lips faster
unless you said
Nature verses...
and yet here you are,
pouring across cauterization.
If your name were onomatopoeia,
I couldn't help but joke about
how hard that must be
to fit on a driver's license.
But we all know that you'd
swim anywhere to put
unfilterable nurture
back in our drinking water.

~ Jon Freeland

Let Us Build Bridges

Human beings have a tendency to fear anything they
    don't understand
or that challenges the beliefs that they already had
A lot of times they take that fear and express it with
    anger or judgment
And then between them grows hatred and resentment
    But what an incredible world this could be
If we didn't let our cognitive dissonance separate you
    and me
If we listen to each other with an understanding ear
Instead digging in our heals and feeding the fear
We don't have to have the same thoughts or believe
    the same things
We just have to accept that all experiences are worthy
    of being seen
Everything has a lesson in which we can learn from
    different hosts
But when we build those walls up we stunt our own growth
So let's build bridges and agree where we can
Like do harm to none and when you see that harm take
    a stand
Let's build bridges to a better tomorrow
Where humanity can grow out of this sorrow
Where we can have love and compassion abound
Where the stories of others become more than a
    background sound.
Let us find empathy for all walks of life

And let us come together to do what we can for those
    spiraling in strife
To lift one another as the tribes used to do
For if we had lived their life we would be them too.

~ Ashley Rae

Secret Boy

We lost you that August back to school sales slow slur of
baseball broadcasts wildflower clusters like paint spilled
over brown Missouri prairie there were so many people to
call your sisters had only just forgiven us and decided you
might fit in there were naming wars in the evenings side-
eye declarations of who you would favor most (of course
it would have been me) it is never anything good when the
doctor leads with I'm sorry words that can actually be seen
trailing from slow-motion mouth even softly spoken even
tenderly intended still arcing with menace toward unready
ears how many times have you been born since that day
incubated in the shelter of my imagination milkfed by your
mother's wish memory A and S sometimes glance down as
we pose for family portraits we know they wonder I mourn
you in wild children's stories like those I improvised when
A and S were small ukulele ringing minor chords voice
rising and falling a preacher a Sesame Street preacher I
give my stories to students in the library now choosing the
best behaved as main characters I wish just once I could
see your eyes astonished as I reveal near the end you are
the secret brave one you are the one who returns through
hidden trapdoor it is you who visits the cobwebby dark
underneath and returns fists full of everything that was
taken

~ Justin Hamm

9/9/2024

The children teach themselves new signs of community.
Too few elders survived the fight to teach them what
    came before.
The children are told they are
too.
loud.
That they take up too.
much.
space.
That they don't know.
That no one like them came before.
It certainly feels like that.
Looking for elders long lost,
long dead too soon.
What would they say if they could see these children?
Still desperately fighting.
Would they be proud?
Would they weep?
What would they think, if anyone had cared enough to
    try for them?
Diana treated like a crazy person,
shaking a hand.
Community born anew,
clinging to the remnants of elders stolen.

~ T.K.Pierce

No Daisies Today

I listened to that AM country station
As it crackled in time to the electric
Fence, and the singer sang about giving
A daisy a day. I remembered the
Countless times you would throw on
The brakes as we drove down F, coming
Home from camping on Cole Camp
Creek. Mom would wonder out loud if
You had lost your mind, but you would
Say not a word until you had run to the
Ditch, picked one of those white pieces of the
Countryside and returned to the car,
Singing the refrain, "I'll give you a
Daisy a day, dear, I'll give you a daisy
A day." Mom would joke that you were
Crazy and quietly smile at the sweet
Smell of love she got from those simple
Petals as she held them to her nose.

I listened to the singer's words,
And I knew there would be no
Daisies again this year.

~ m. pottorff

Apology to my ~~Ex-Girlfriends~~
Dead Houseplants

I was not able to keep
any of you alive. Never
planted deep. Not
enough sunlight or water.

No opportunity to properly
root, pessimistic at the first
sign of leaves browning
or stems drooping.

Soon uprooted completely,
every time
replaced with
fresh greenery.

I really
did want you
to flourish: but
there was this tree.

Planted seedling grew
for many years, I tended—
tall enough for shade
and sheltering children.

Then—rotting limbs.
The children left.
I was left,
sawing branches.

Even though I knew you
needed a gardener,
a partner to share
the sunlight.

~ Rick Christiansen

Cooking Rice

A long journey
in a rumbling truck to a ship
contained in container darkness
weak from thirst.

Sea sickness survived
she doubts now the promise
made to her parents
as they pressed bills
into a stranger's hand.

In a filthy room with others
who survived
realizing the ropes
around her wrists
she turns to face a girl next to her.

A pasty fat man
with a camera says
be nice act happy
perform look hopeful
you could get lucky move to Florida.

This future pushes in
points on the horizon
blur and recede
she closes her eyes and pretends
knowing there will be no other hereafter
no family no love only long
and lonely longing.

When the deed is done
and the needle applied
she sinks into forgetfulness.

the screams of her bedmate fade
she is back in the Philippines
with the family
cooking rice.

~ Sharon SingingMoon Feltman

I Fear Me This - Is Loneliness

-Emily Dickinson, *"The Loneliness One dare not sound-"*

Emily, you sought your solitude
at your desk by a bedroom window,
composing poems and letters to the world
that never wrote to you.
My room, a solitary sanctuary
with a view to the street.
I compose notes with blessings
to lift others up during this tender time
of ire and illness.
Your seclusion, Emily, chosen
from grief and loss.
Mine, too, as I hear of deaths.
Families felled by COVID.
Strain after strain.
Again and again.
Occasionally you lowered
baked goods in baskets to children
celebrating innocent sun.
I watch children in our neighborhood park
attempt a great escape
down small slopes of ice
to the creek.
Outside your winter sky
hid cold birds in a haze
like the masks we should wear these days
to spare our lives.
You wished to help one fainting robin
Unto his nest again.

At my window daily, a solitary robin
smacks his body into his own reflection.
Repeatedly – My fear of death
mutates into chaos.
For you, Emily,
a garden of grief bloomed
a leather-bound herbarium. Sorrow plucked
and pressed between flimsies.
On my notes and poems, I press stickers
of wildflowers and butterflies. My handwriting
meanders in my tiny gardens of verse
that snail mail delivers to loved ones
in pearly shells.
Our windows – glassy protection from what waits
in the soul's Caverns and its Corridors
that can Illuminate-or seal-.
As our stars rage their light
into gossamer tears –
our pens open
many doors.

~ Barbara Leonhard

TEARS IN A BOTTLE

Maya said every storm runs out of rain. Perhaps, but I don't think so. My bottle is full of tears, wet and salty. I have been saving my tears since you went away. I collect them when no one is watching.

Sometimes they come in a flood and there is no way to not waste some. They overflow the spout, slide down the sides and drip on my shoes. Sometimes they slowly roll down my face and I capture every one .

My bottle is full of tears but I am dying of thirst for your touch, for that smile and the twinkle in your eyes. I so miss, that knowing look that passes between old lovers.

I miss the sound of your voice. That little giggle when you say "I would like a kiss from the handsome man in the red beret." I liked it when your foot would find my leg in the middle of the night, just to be sure I was still there.

It is still raining in my storm, and I have a bottle full of tears.

~ John Clayton

Poetry Reading with Approaching Storm

We switched off the phones
when they began blaring
weather warnings –
the clouds and the wind
spoke clearly enough:
the sudden rush of cool air,
the ominous darkening
of the sky, the breeze
that picked up papers
and last year's leaves.
We grasped our books tighter,
felt the first sprinkles.
Determined, we held out
until heavy drops splashed
and we rushed, laughing,
inside the old farmhouse.
Settled in the snug room,
with its dark beams and white-
washed walls, we read on,
with the door open
to the drumming of rain
and, later, the frog calls,
and the spring smell
of wet earth.

~ Agnes Vojta

Cicadas

There is something very American Gothic
    about listening to the cicadas scream as the day
    draws down dark.
About the moments before a big storm,
where the damp heat is curling in your head like a fist
    and the cicadas are screaming.
There is thunder in the distance, and they shriek defiance
    of their lives.
For days after 17 years of waiting, the cicadas scream.
We are here.
We are alive.
The storm cannot stop us.

~ T.K. Pierce

Mist Aches

for T.K.

It makes sense that we store our lives
in the cloud, always within reach
but just distant enough
to make everything "tut tut…"
Functionality is the expectation,
emoshunacceptable.
"FIX YOUR FACE!"
So I absorb the mist aches
and mockingword
until I blurred it out.
Now that everyone's looking,
it's only window pain,
drowning by the thrillians
in shallow pond, er
running like downloaded Dali
under brief bridges
and I don't have to just
get
over
it.

~ Jon Freeland

Overcoming my triggers

Oh no, a trigger
So what are you gonna do
Sit here and wish the past didn't happen to you
Dwell in self-pity
Rage at everyone else
Project onto others
How about take accountability for yourself
Sorry to say,
You can't change the past
And holding onto the pain
Will ruin your future happiness
So how are you gonna let go
How do you plan to move on
How many times
Do we have to play this tired old song
You're infinite energy
A being without end
Your flesh one day will rot off
And then will it matter where it's been
Will it matter what was done
Will it matter who betrayed you
No, the only thing that will matter is
What you chose to do
Let go of expectations
Of how others should be
Release them to be themselves
And if that hurts you set them free
Because those meant for you
Will dwell within your boundaries

What you need from them
Will be who they are naturally
Stop overthinking
And getting in your own mind
Trust in the divine process
I promise everything turns out just fine.

~ Ashley Rae

Tucson Sketches - #1 Neighbors

We glimpse the coyote
slinking through the neighborhood,
its lean mangy body slipping between
our houses at twilight—noiseless,

humorless—a scrawny thing
& hard to love, like someone else's
newborn: a little red, a little hungry.
I've seen it lurking among the hedgerows

of bougainvillea that pour like falling water
into our yards, scavenging the detritus
accumulating there, dependent
on our kindness, & no regard

for our personal affections. You & I
wave as we pass, your chihuahua bobbing
its head from your purse, trembling
in the heat, a world of misery escaping

its eyes as you soothe its forehead,
its ears, with your thumb,
a phone pressed to your ear.
And in the late afternoon, I've seen you

slide your patio door a crack, the pup fleeing
for a moment of privacy, its toes clicking
across the concrete patio bare feet won't touch,
passing the lantana spindling its pinks & whites

from clay pots, heading out into the gravel
toward the wide umbrella of the grapefruit tree
to scratch like a dog in the sinewy rinds
of last winter's excess. I've watched you allow it

out of your line of sight, shaking off a passing
cloud of anxiety under those azure skies
like a flip of your hair—if only
for a moment, knowing the risk.

Because the coyote is loveless & edgy,
hunkering, masked in the scenery, ready
to meet what moves with a mute swipe
to the head—a brushstroke captured

in a DeGrazia painting—sweeping
the neck into those jaws, as agile
as a champion, then carrying it somewhere
you won't go looking, through the arroyos

the Spanish named the Rillito & the Santa Cruz—
the little river & the holy cross—
then out into the sharp lushness
of the Sonoran Desert where we hear

the unholy howl, the gathering call,
& the pack yipping to the heavens
before taking their communion, before
the mauve skies strike against the Santa Catalinas

& the darkness washes out the day.

~ Cortney Daniels

Carrying the World in a Broken
Laundry Basket

Isn't easy to do on steep basement stairs.
The basket, filled with the bemired nightmares of the day
stubbornly sticking to threads.

We're instructed to separate the colors – Why?
Lest they bleed together onto the pristine sheets
worn to the rallies?
Tide Pods. FDA approved for COVID yet?
Is bleach required for stained smiles
behind the masks?

How many cycles are needed
for the urine-soiled carpet
from the U.S. Capitol Building? Can it fit
into my Sears washer, or is it dry clean only?

Mother always admonished,
Never use the flag pole
To beat the rugs!

She'd fuss about this flag,
frayed by the spinning
Spinning, tossing and turning
In the fury of the moment
as red puddles spread their arms
on the white and blue.

Is it illegal to hang the wash in the backyard
at half-mast?

I hear that folding laundered funds is an art.
Money runs in hot water. Instructions in fine print,
Use Free and Clear. Lay flat 'til dry.

The overloaded washing machine packs heat.
Makes its rounds.
Ratatatat! Ratatatat!
Ratatatat! Ratatatat!

A shoe caught in the pant leg
Kicks the dryer wall to the step,
Thump. Thump. Thump. Thump.
The dryer wheezes. I pull lint
from the ventilator. Press restart.
Then add softener to the last load of hearts.

~ Barbara Leonhard

Heart felt

I put the laundry in the dryer
and remember the day we strolled
through the town after lunch,
not ready to say goodbye.
The years of absence
had fallen away like dust
in a breeze. Confidences
came easy. We wandered
into a store that sold soaps
and wooden brushes. A glass jar
with felted dryer balls
stood on the windowsill. I told you
how the dogs had claimed
my old one as a toy. You picked
a ball with a rainbow heart
and bought it for me.
I watched your car disappear
down the road. We forgot
to take a picture. But I smile
and think of you when I open my dryer.

~ Agnes Vojta

Inhale / Exhale

Inhale
In death
Exhale.
Last Breath.
Cringe
At light
Peace
During Blight
Pain engulfs
Pain fuels
Pain recedes
Pain becomes numb
Numb to pain
Numb to hurt
Numb from anger
Numb to sorrow
Numbness becomes
Silence
Silence needs
Isolation
Isolation is
Safe
Isolation is
Death
Darkness consumes
Isolation
Like a plague
Darkness becomes
Sanctuary

Death becomes
Freedom
Death is release
And Dark is safe

Exhale
Past strife
Inhale
New life
Embrace
Possibilities
In love
Just breathe
Joys heal
Passions run
Play ignites
Light has won
Light is hope
Light is exciting
Light is love
Light is smiling
A true smile
One from within
Never to be harmed
Or humiliated again
Safety and stability
Secure in life
Dreams never dared
Become Monday nights
Life becomes beauty
Life becomes sacred
Life becomes anything

Without fear
New Friendships
New love
Strengthen
what was
To become
What is

~ A. Rae

First Dawn

All that is,
all that we know to be true,
would not, could not, be
without a beginning,
that moment of birth
as senses were awakened
by the light of the first dawn,
the nothing of before forsaken.

Darkness, the past
that never was,
left behind in an instant
for the unknown,
a promise of a future
that life would hold more,
the chance to experience
the possibilities in store.

And what possibilities
they are. No guarantees,
but potential. For good.
Or bad. Taken
one day at a time.
Understanding, learning
from life's lessons.
Always discerning.

Long forgotten,
that first dawn,
yet we understand
that each new day
offers the same,
holds the potential
for a meaningful life,
knowledge that is essential.

~ Ken Gierke

Patty

When my life seemed
At its darkest,
You have been my light.

As he lay dying,
You held my hand and
Gave me strength on the
Journey back home.

When she fell so quickly,
You were my rock and
My support - to keep me
From falling apart.

And when that simple surgery
Went so wrong, you were there,
Holding my hand again and keeping
Me strong, even at the point of despair.

I am stronger than I should be
And more than I could be,
Because you have loved me.

~ m. pottorff

Last Light

A trying day
pressing close to its end,
I watch your sleep,
restless for both of us.

Eyes closed,
do you see what lies
ahead or a past
that is out of reach

but seems closer
the closer you come
to being with the one
you've held dear?

When a calm settles
over you, I leave
to find my own
beside the river.

Sun low on the horizon,
its rippled reflection
is no match for the light
that once filled your eyes.

In the sun's last light,
a cool breeze off the water
is no substitute
for a mother's caress.

Night upon us,
I return to your side
to face the inevitable,
your hand in mine.

~ Ken Gierke

It Was A Good Day

There's a phrase I don't hear very often,
let alone think or feel for myself

It rolled off his tongue so easily, so smoothly.
The more I thought about it though,
He was right.

It had, in fact, been
a bright, Sunshine-y day.

~ Caitlin Korte

Sleepwalking the Sunset Circus

With a huddle of hula hoops
skimming its hips and one foot

gripping the seat, a yellow bear
rides into sunset on my first bicycle,

the one my dad spray-painted
for me when I was six.

I love its dented fenders,
plastic streamers, and the memory

of it hanging on ceiling hooks
with newspaper beneath, dad's

index finger red against the nozzle,
the smell of blue in our noses,

and the swell of silly that made him
open the basement window.

~ Lynne Jensen Lampe

Writer's Retreat: Haibun

Marietta booked the remote villa hoping to finish her manuscript. She couldn't yet admit that she liked picturing herself as an author far more than she liked the actual work of crafting words. *I've spent the last two years making excuses,* she sighed. Six months later, her writing career on hold yet again, we find her humming along at dawn in the herb garden. Then workmen are already in full swing renovating her villa down the winding road toward the village, the one with the red mailbox and sunflower yellow walls. Soon she'll open her pensione and retreat center. Then she'll begin turning the outbuildings into a culinary school and bakery. Overseeing the details will keep her busy for at least five years. The vision had blessedly overtaken her while she was gazing out the window across lush hillsides, trying to find the exact words to describe warm breezes rippling sunflowers like a tidal pool.

at last she begins
world-class procrastinator
summer dawn rising

~ Cam Whelr MD

A Little Jam

She said, "Wait, before you go."
Seeking clarity, she finds
the toast is burnt
buttering may not save it.

She said, "Running is always an option."
Cracking eggs into hot oil
she moves away from
angry splatters.

She said, "Closeness can be dangerous."
Spilling sugar around her cup
hot coffee fragrance
fills the kitchen.

She said, "Burnt edges just need a little jam."
Spooning last summer's goodness
over this morning's
imperfections.

~Sharon SingingMoon Feltman

For Love

I thought of stars bursting overhead
the summer my belly enlarged
like the sun on the horizon
growing in the morning.
I grazed your side
with my breathing. I loved
the indulgence & your hands
& arms around me in sleep.

That was time, time wound around us
like a coil in a clock now obsolete.
No hands are needed to mark our time;
the long memories are put up inside—
jelly in a cellar. We've worn each other
down like well-used toys with no spare parts.
Yet, had you no mouth, I'd know you
as a shout roaring through my body.

*

We've made a whole city of this life.
The load-bearing walls are crumbling
& the I-beams are going up. In the dawn,
the facades emerge, grids of them.
Beyond us, we see the sketchy outline
of a harbor & a lake to cool in.
While you're out pacing the streets
in the mornings, I float around the moorings—
the heart tethered wherever it may go. I've grown

lazy in my loving. And when I dry
myself, & moisten for the bed,
I hold back my kisses.

I think of time in all the rooms
where our children played.
I think of all the words gone
into us, words circling this house
from beginning to end
or hanging like a plumb bob
where nothing can align.

As we lose each other
I work at keeping time.
For love, we made this record—
back in the soft days
when we pierced each other
& made our good impressions.
Hear it play now—its crackles, its
unforgiving scratches, the staccatos,
& this skipping, skipping
through time.

~ Cortney Daniels

Flowerbed

"What sort of flower are you?"
How can one possibly know, when petals stand in the sun
    out of sight?
When roots grow deeper and deeper, hiding everything
    that keeps me alive.
How can I think of what sort of flower I am in a flurry
    of vivid yellows, rushing purples?
How can I look within?
I cannot know what I am, living among the joyful riot.

~ T.K. Pierce

The Goddess and the Sea

the goddess lays at the banks
of the deep blue sea
feeling the wet sand
as her fingers grasp beneath

the tide brings the water
as it laps at her skin
as it comes forth
and then retreats again

the bubbles pop
as the tide washes over
sending tingling sensations
kissing her like a lover

Charging each chakra
Bring balance to the chaos
Energizing and healing
the pain within the Goddess

So that when she rises
She rises in light
She rises in love
She rises in all her glorious might

For she is a goddess
and nothing will prevent
The love she's meant to spread
The light she's called to send

~ A. Rae

Dragon, in Flight

wings beat, move
in a rhythm that is mystery

my patience tested
as I follow

here, there, wondering
at the rhythm of my paddle

current of water
my consolation for air

left, right, sunlight favored
trees and shaded waters forsaken

always in the light, shadows
no substitute for hindrance

on the hunt, with quarry
that hovers in the summer heat

my presence limited to
the cooler water

tantalizing as it alights
on the bow of my kayak

a dragonfly, elusive
even as it hesitates

breaking from its hunt,
only to be captured by my lens

~ Ken Gierke

For the Fairies: Haibun

We spend all afternoon together, you charmed by the fairy garden and begging to leave the fairies small gifts: a carrot, three raisins, a stick of celery, half a pecan, a blueberry. Then you hide, watching, waiting. It's your third visit hoping to spy them flying home at dusk, because that's when fairies are most likely. You already love them, though they're yet to appear.

Moonrise scribbles

Please, I'd like some wings.

Hope they don't itch.

~ Cam Whelr MD

Blue Bird of Happiness

the British royals own the English swans
they are the only ones allowed to catch, cook & eat them
though their dietary whims have changed
the royals still claim proprietary rights
by way of royal birth
wrongs, atrocities of the past
that brought their ancestors to the throne
now seem forgotten by some

in my garden skies are clear
blue birds explore birdhouses
make plans for nesting, they are vulnerable
as aggressive sparrows & starlings
compete for food, raid their nests
pierce the eggs with their beaks

the British gave away what was not theirs
now Palestine is choked with toxic smoke
there are no birds in Gaza
spring skies swarm with drones & bombs
mothers & fathers write their names
on their babies' arms so they will be
known if found dead under the rubble

my arms long to cradle the starving children
faces smeared with blood, stained with ash
eyes just staring, they tremble
have seen too much, lost everything
everyone they love is dead

spring comes warm & wet in my garden
daffodils slip silently from their winter sleep
I hang birdhouses from tree branches

~ Sharon SingingMoon Feltman

Small Talk

One of my favorite poets says "everything but I love you
is small talk"

I thought I agreed...

But what if I love you and am afraid that saying it will
take our small talk away?

It's our small talk that led the way to genuine loving
feelings
Small talk a compass letting me know I'm going in the
right direction
Along the path of small talk I arrived at a deep
knowing—I love you
I love you, and I'm wildly uncertain about our destination
Both things can be true—love and uncertainty
I have been afraid to say I love you so I keep to the small
talk that I also love so much, they're both so beautifully
entangled
We both know that our small talk is not always so small

I swim in gratitude for the small talk that told me who
you are

Small talk with a strong undercurrent of love

If the destination involves a broken heart one day, I trust
that no time will have been wasted
You've shown me a beautiful sliver of light that affirms
what I want in a partner is out there

The feelings of I love you don't scare me anymore
The fear is attached to saying these words out loud and
    having something about us unravel
I'm not scared of the love I have for you—I am scared
    that those words will scare you

I think I've been too afraid to say I love you so I write about
    how I might love you instead gently tiptoeing around it

I love you, I love the small talk, I love it all
I even love that this could end, and I trust I'd make it through
    the wilderness of grief with gratitude and fond memories
    of our precious, precious small talk

    ~ Keely Alexander

Triple Word Score

I dream that we are playing Scrabble on the phone.
Word games from a distance.

Arguing over the EXACT placement of each tile.
It is so important to us both
that no cheating occur.

I imagine your look of concentration as you search
    through
your alphabet for the right combination of letters to
    unlock
the secret of the board.

Winning is not your goal.
You just want to make a good impression.

> ~ Rick Christiansen

Untitled

Do you remember that song,
where the guy told us to trust him on the sunscreen?
He had a line in there about
remembering the compliments we receive
and forgetting the insults.
We were supposed to tell him how, if we ever figured
that out.

I think it's a mix. We inevitably carry both.
The things that were recited at us,
to us.
Hurtful things lobbed, with and without thought.
Silly phrases that cannot be lived without.

I took his weird words, translated them into a dead language;
in an attempt to make them my own ... and tattooed
them on my body.
It's on my back though.
Sometimes I forget they are there.
But when I do remember, it is comforting.
Weird and a little uncomfortable, being rooted in him ...
but the sentiment stands.
I am stronger than I know.

They all bubble up. Some randomly, some cruelly, others
with ridiculous comedic timing.

"More water, less salt."
"Breathe on top of the water."

"Stupidity should be painful."
"This is why we work hard and save, so we can afford to take care of ourselves."

She had a thing for Emerson,
"That which lies behind us, and that which lies before us ..."
"I'm just your parent, I don't know anything."
"How are you ever going to find one of your own, if you're spending all your time with someone else's?"

"Pay for your own comfort."

"Only if you're good."

"Oodles and oodles and noodles and lots."

"EXTREME!"
"Wildly not to scale."

~ Caitlin Korte

Judging

for Caitlin

He'd hate that I titled it like that.
It may be among his least favorite
of public things about himself.
I can relate, non sequiter.
Most seats are self-elected,
selected because solitude is easier,
low skies, even short arms can
scrape up a blanket never quite
tight enough to foil
precipitation, it does not follow.
Devon and Cornwallowing,
hot hands hard to hold
sweat, refuse to melt
lost to the ages (and Steve Perry)
only fold when they find you waiting.
On days like giving all I can,
they pull out all that you put in my box,
Dawning, when you can't follow.
They are reminders
that I'm not a Vedder man,
that our snares move and don't trap
in tarmac river flows.
Somehow, you want to go
even where I don't,
Judging.

Reading. Remembering.
I think I could conquer anything,
so long as you're there holding my hand.

~ Jon Freeland

On Warm Days in Winter

On warm days in winter,
with serene caerulean skies above,
northwest winds laid down low
across the lately cut corn fields
and sunbeams gleam
through the skeletal tracery branches
of the hardwoods, their twisted shadows
settling dark upon the dried buff-colored grasses
knee-deep at the edge of old pastures
where horses stand long shadowed
their rough shaggy coats warmed
in the bright clear chromatic light,
those very perfect afternoons
together
my friend
between Christmas and New Year's
we both
back home, trekking up old traces
into the hills whilst the dogs ran free.
We looked out at boundless blue skies
reflecting on the wide flow of our forever
running river, never to think of days ahead
when these things for us might
end.

~ Jude MacAllen-Tatman

Exposure

He loves the slow and lonely work.
In the orange glow, he watches
shadows grow on the paper,
darkening shapes blossom.
From his test prints, he knows
how long the photo needs to soak
in the developer, when to move
it to the stop bath, to the fixer.

At the end of the day, ten portraits
will hang on the drying line:
acrobats, jugglers, stilt-walkers,
dancers – street performers, captured

mid-flow. He dislikes poses,
and circus acts that are now
all about break-neck speed.
Speed is not important to him.
He bicycles, travels by train,
eschews the subway, walks instead
unbothered by his luggage – how
can he see if he is underground?

He does not show his photographs.
They cover the walls in his house:
clowns, mimes, and fire-eaters, none
looking towards the audience.

~ Agnes Vojta

Not a Hero

Just not yet shattered
Reflecting and bending light
We are all new glass

My father was past 80 when he finally began to tell us
    about the war.
It was his first war, when he was only 20.
He served during three conflicts.
But it was that first war that marked him.

It started when we found the box of his medals and
we told him that he was a hero.
He became angry. He rejected the label with scorn.
He told us…

That he knew heroic men.
But that he was not one of them.
He said…

First you get scared and you stay scared.
You are frightened for so long and so relentlessly.

That you get angry and you stay angry.
You are angry for so long and so relentlessly.

That you get stupid.
You start to take risks.
You do crazy things that you would never have imagined.

And if those crazy things don't get you killed,
well then, they give you medals.

But it was all just because you were afraid.
And you didn't want to be there.
You could not believe that you WERE there.
How the hell did it happen?

You were pissed at yourself, and the enemy, and your
   mission,
and the cold, and the dirt and the bullets, and the
   goddam army!

He said the good war movies got a lot of it right.
At least the newer ones.
But he said they couldn't get at his deepest memory of
   it all.

The smell.

He told us of the smell of his own skin
and of the men around him in the foxholes.

Once they had a break.
The Major told them to put the torn and worn uniforms
   that they had been wearing for months into a pile.
A gigantic pile of filthy fabric.
And they doused it with kerosene to burn the stench
   and the lice.
And they all got cold showers.
And fresh uniforms were on the way.

But the new uniforms never got there.
Each man had to pick through the pile of kerosene
   soaked garments.

Trying to find something close to the right size.
With correct rank and insignia.

He said he spent two more months in another man's
    clothes.
And that it took a week before the stink was his own again,
even through the stench of kerosene.
But they were grateful.
At least the fuel killed the lice.

He said the cold that winter was worse than the artillery.
The shells came in waves.
There were lulls and valleys in the action.
But the cold was constant.

He said you got worried if it stopped hurting.
That meant the cold was winning.
So you would shake and stomp to bring back the pain
that told you that you were still alive.

And then he showed us his three belly buttons from the
    bullet wounds.
But this time he wasn't being silly like every time before.
This time he was in earnest.
For the first time he was bearing witness.
It wasn't a punchline anymore.

He told us all of these things almost quietly.
Quickly, and with an embarrassment bordering on shame.
But also some stubborn pride.

He just wanted us to know.

That he was not a hero.
You see.

~ Rick Christiansen

TELL THEM

I have their names, addresses and phone numbers in my journal. They are there because of a sacred promise I made. A promise made to their sons, their grandsons, and nephews. A promise made because that young man believed that a personal contact from me to their loved one would somehow ease their pain and grief.

If I don't make it.

Tell them I loved them
Tell them I was a good person.
Tell them I didn't kill anybody.
Tell them I wasn't scared

Tell them I was brave.
Tell them I didn't cry.
Tell them I didn't suffer.
Tell them I talked about them

Tell them I carried candy for kids.
Tell them I loved my little brother and sister.
Tell them to keep taking care of my dog, Clifford.
Tell them I will miss them too.

Tell them I love our country and it's worth it.
Tell them I will see them up there.
Tell them this war don't mean nothing.

Yeah, I will call them. Yeah, I will go see them. I will tell them they were all you talked about. I will tell them they should be proud of you. I will tell them you were kind and good.

I won't mention that you shot the kid who threw that satchel charge. I will forget that time you froze up and I had to pull your ass out of that ditch to get on the chopper.

No problem, buddy. I will tell them anything to make them feel better. I know you would do it for me. That's what we do. We take care of each other. That IS what we do.

~ John Clayton

G(r)avel

for John

In standing guarden
between dirt and crusher run,
dusty eyes make mud.

~ Jon Freeland

PonDurance

So much pre
goes into the ponderance.
All that evidence
just throwing its weight around.

But what about the post?
Why is the post so lacking
in that pon durance?
Why are the before
and during
somehow more worthy
of that same endurance?

Isn't it more likely
that we'll end up spending
far more time
with the effects of the post,
than we ever did
in the presence of the
pre or the ponderance?

~ Caitlin Korte

Disjuncted: a study in Living with Chemo-brain

…my coffee went cold while looking for one of my
 slippers
            when my brother called to tell me Bob had
    died.
he was old. he'd been sick a long time. Parkinson's
            —he wanted me to come to the funeral—
my brother that is. not Bob. Bob doesn't give a shit. i said
            he's dead. he won't know i'm not there.
WHERE THE FUCK'S MY COFFEE? but the boys
    will be there,
            he said, they will ask about you/me/ i told
him hold on– my coffee mug; where the hell is it?
            It's next to that stack of books, she said
as she came into the room. *Please straighten this up,*
            she asked looking at the table. I don't have
room on my desk; the research is too voluminous.
            Nice big word, she snarked love in her voice
as it trailed out the door. i pour some cold coffee from
            the French press into the mug. what was
i doing? preparing to sit down to read Ulysses
            S. Grant. sat the mug down. the goddamned
phone rang; actually it quacks. the dogs' favorite
            ringtone. they come running as soon as it
starts to ring/quack. she hates it. says it's annoying–
            sounds kind of redneck. well, we do own bird
dogs.
I do hunt birds. that we eat. when I was healthy. some
    snobs
            think that is redneck. I used to hunt birds

with my brother. why was he was calling? I answered
   only
            because it was him. why was he calling?
in the middle of the day? someone must've– no– died
            otherwise, the phone can quack its fucking
ass off. for fuck's sake MacAllen where in the HELL IS
            THE FUCKING PHONE? retrace my path to
the kitchen counter. there. by the tea kettle. and *Fuck!*
            he hung up. two texts. 1: Call me back about
Bob. 2. *Don't forget your oncology appt. @ 3:15*
            need errands ran after that. i'll text a list.
I collapse into the Morris chair. one foot is still cold.
            what the fuck did those dogs do with my
other slipper?
            where's my fucking coffee mug?
Goddamnit.
            Bob died.

            ~ Jude MacAllen-Tatman

Quiet is the Longest Sentence

for Allen

Did you know that prime numbers
plotting on polar coordinates
start scattered and then become
spirals, then as healing distance, rays?
My relationship with radiation
has not always been the best.
They say poison is my crucible, but there were
no snakes or snails in my bastible,
only hell and high fire water.
Neither age nor chemical steals my vision,
but I lay my spectacle on ash table:
Haze is a deal I made with myself to never look
when I could make a blind world better.
As drop slides down to trickle, he's running into spring,
falling to his knees under amniotic lazy river,
Queen Anne's Lace full of Black-eyed Susan
standing watch, lifeguard and reminder to lose yourself
so you can billow from Cattails.
I rain dance for radiance,
just one prime number
itself a galaxy too far away
to be seen as anything other
than a point in a plot.
In my radius, I shine.
Close enough, and I swirl,
closer still and I scatter, a multiverse on tiptoes.

We are, perhaps far beyond our winter,

finding the win within

because or despite

living is dying tomorrow.

~ Jon Freeland

We Six

As the family grieved their
   loss one more time,
Charlie solemnly closed
   the lid,
And the family went
   to their cars.
The six of us lined up
   like we were told,
Tallest to shortest,
   three on each side,
The double doors opened,
   and we took him to his
   car.
On the way out there we made
   jokes to break the tension --
      "Wouldn't the old ladies
      throw a fit if we went to
      a drive-in liquor store."
We did this and remembered him
   the four miles out there.
When we got there,
   the whole procession moved
Up the hill, but we stayed
   below.
Charlie told us, "Take
   it slow boys, and don't fall."

They opened the door,
and we six grandsons
Carried our Grandpa to
his grave.

~ m. pottorff

Limestone

For millions of years, rainwater percolated through rotting
leaves. Turned acidic, it seeped through the cracks
and fissures of limestone bedrock, both solid and dissolvable.

Now, a lightless land, an anti-earth, lies underfoot the Ozarks.
When we walk the wooden paths of a state park,
or float beneath an overhang on a crystal stream,

we know, beneath us, is a world that both frightens and
soothes. Who hasn't stood at the mouth of a cave, and
paused? It's a deep fault within us, the twin wants, one to flee

into the sun, the other, to lose ourselves in the wandering
darkness. I think what draws us to caves is that what makes a
cave a cave is what is not there. We desire an ontology of
    absence.

But absence is one thing that can never be. This is what we
fear: our tears, turned bitter, wore away the certainty of any
ground. We are nothing more than caverns and karsts that
    crisscross

the fissures, crests, depressions, and ridges of our soft
human form. If even the earth cannot be trusted, how much
less can we? Maybe that is why we buried our dead in caves,
    to refill

this emptiness with human flesh and bone and winding sheets.
I like to believe that when we touch moist cave walls,
those are tears of the dead, in their decay, all the more solid.

~ Richard Stimac

Memory Bank

Scattered, like the gray matter
that assigns them value,
their significance lost to
most observers, are
the things I treasure.

Gallon jars filled with beach glass
collected on the shore of Lake Ontario.
Anchors and bottles, some of them clay,
all used and discarded before my time,
found during underwater adventures,
some of my favorite times.

A box filled with negatives
and photos older than most of
my possessions. Hand-colored
wedding photos taken nine months
before my birth. Hundred-year-old
portraits of family I'll never meet,
or meet again, their place
on my walls taken by artwork
from the hands of treasured friends.

A metal cigar box passed on
by my grandfather, holding
items left untouched
for half-a-century. Ink-pen tips.
The nametag from my first job
as a store clerk. A devotional
scapular not worn in sixty-plus

years, a highlight of my youth
even in its insignificance.
It's the metal box that's a treasure.

A spatula held by my mother
as she served pie or cake.
The tiny mission-style table
that once belonged to her
as a teen, that I refinished as a teen,
now sitting beside my recliner.
Tools smoothed by my father's hands
feel comfortable in my own.
The grandfather clock I built
for their anniversary will,
one day, chime for my children.

The band worn on my wrist, a bond
between father and daughter forged
in the health crisis of her early years.
A stained-glass frame and its photo,
a father's pride in three broad smiles.
A canvas print of two people joined
in marriage beside a lighthouse
on the shore of Lake Erie.

As scattered as my memories can be,
the value of my treasures is magnified
by the memories they hold. The closer
I hold them, the longer I hold on to
those memories, my greatest treasure.

~ Ken Gierke

That Crazy Old Lady

still has her Christmas tree up!
Indeed! Been three years now.
The LED lights haven't failed to sparkle
at passersby walking their dogs
and children playing in the park.

The few music students continuing
since COVID struck
blink several times
as they arrive weekly for lessons
to see the tree still waiting
for more Bluegrass tunes.

The bluebird pecking
at the picture window each spring -
Does it want to nest
in the tree's brilliant branches
alongside the crystalline angels
and shimmering orbs

on artificial branches?
My tree, fake news? Hardly.
As my gaze rests there,
I'm spared headlines of disease,
mass shootings, bombs marked
"For the Children", the inflictions
of 'isms', the forays of fear.

My Christmas tree,
determined to stand
until kindness and forgiveness
light up this world again.

~Barbara Leonhard

Blues Healer

for Jason Ryberg

Nihilism isn't a just a river in Egypt.
It is specks on glasses,
obstacles that only exist while seaing.
It is no accident that the opposite of orient is occident,
or is it?
"Did you know that scars are constant
ly being rebuilt
with collagen?
Sailors with scurvy would watch their wounds open
because their bodies couldn't keep up.
Then there were limeys."
How many eyebrows had to perennially
bloom before healthy bitterness stemmed bodily mutiny?
"What is a poem?"
Wry grin side eye beginning 10 o'clock
coffee mocking definition, shockingly not
letter of the law.
"The real question is what does it do?
Does it half to tell the truth or is the story
better than real"
now that the movie, music, lyric, stadium stars
killed…the stars
and they blamed Courtney,
Yoko, Mary Kate, Asia, Jada,
cocaine, whiskey, pride…
"I didn't know you were an academic."
Like midwest paddington, he adjusted a purposely
crooked brim and his smile belies

the swagger drawl in "a lawwwng time agooo…" like low
organ drone
in the corner of Barb's, memories of the dusty setting
button depression,
how it shucked like grandma's old Wurlitzer otherwise
silent, lids mostly closed
listening to redeye spoken pictures
and I realize that you need
lies to spell limes.
Dirty hands tell the best stories
and mine can't help but thumbbleed
so they can mend.

~ Jon Freeland

A Squirrel's Front Teeth Never Stop Growing

Mom foraged for meals for nine daily. She hunted for
quilt patterns and party dresses for teen girls. She gathered
sea shells to glue to our gift baskets. She organized our
puzzle pieces by colors and shapes. She sorted socks of all
sizes and seasons. She stashed pennies to invest in Dad's
retirement. Our nest was always a crowded mess.

One by one, we fell out
and scurried away
to our own trees.

Dad squirreled away all his childhood toys and family
heirlooms. To haul from nest to nest. His old red metal
truck. His mother's doilies and kitchen utensils. His father's
tools. Even his old college papers and letters. But my toys,
paintings, and memo pads with my poems. Discarded at
the base of old tree homes.

My dreams, abandoned
for strangers to scavenge
and rain to drown.

~ Barbara Leonhard

Upon Hearing of My Untimely End,
I Write a Poem to the Mother Who
Never Knew Me

". . .it wasn't obvious she was pregnant.
Her mother sent her to Montreal.
. . . knew it was a girl . . . told me she had died."

From notes my found brother shared with me
after a phone conversation
with my mother's best friend.

in memoriam: Marie Noella Aline Mackay (8/1931-10/2003)
for my half-brother, Bill Spurge (7/1956-2/2021)

It's six o'clock;
dead babies don't talk.
Neither day nor dark—
dead babies don't talk.
No more to say—he left that day.
You let him walk.
Dead babies don't talk.

This plan was unwritten. Dead babies
don't quicken. Turn off the spark.
Dead babies don't talk. See in the mirror
your little dark error? Why feed the lie—
dead babies don't cry. Starve yourself—
tarnish the heart. Rub me out—
until death us do part.

You went to term & felt me squirm.
I challenged the order & crossed the border.
Four pounds was enough. It wasn't love.

You heard me squawk. Dead babies don't talk.
The doctors said I had your face—
a kind of smudge you could erase.
Dead babies occupy no space.
You signed me away—your sudden
stranger—because dead babies
pose no danger.

They told you forget it.
Your best friend went quiet.
Don't worry my mother—
I lived & defied it. But you
went one way. I went another.
Dead babies have no chance
with their mother.

No time to recover, you pulled yourself
together, married some New Yorker
(forget her) (forget her).
Made quick a new baby.
Maybe this time was better.
It all turns out. He looks like his father.
His breath brushed your chest
when you held him to rock—
woke the echo, the echo:
dead babies don't talk.

The whole arrangement couldn't last,
You took me with you when you passed.
But you're his mother, & he's my brother.
Nothing stopped us from finding each other.
Membranes will rupture & secrets are borne.

Your despair fed my hunger. Dead babies
come home. Given by you: this girl
so nameless—forgiven by him.
We all can go blameless.

~ Cortney Daniels

I'm Sorry

I'm sorry
I'm sorry I'm me
I'm sorry I speak
I'm sorry I breathe

I'm sorry I'm happy
I'm sorry I'm so annoying
I'm sorry I exist
I'm sorry I'm crying

I'm sorry I laugh
I'm sorry I share
I'm sorry I feel
I'm sorry I care

I'm sorry I can't figure out
The way to behave appropriately
That social situations tend to be
An overwhelming explosion of anxiety

I'm sorry that I can't
That I can't be sorry
For the fact that I exist
Or for just being me

If I bother you that much
It's okay to take space
Because I'm done being sorry
For things I can't change

I'm going to be bold
And speak with confidence
I'm done discrediting my own knowledge
Because you don't understand it

I am both light and dark
Strength and Vulnerability
Compassion and boundaries
My goal is authenticity

With my words I will express
The joys and sorrows of this existence
I will speak my truth
And no longer be silenced

I will not make myself small
Because you can't handle that truth
I also will not be fake
Just to appease you

I've come to understand
Life's so much more than that nightmare
I'm done being sorry
I'm done being scared

Because yes, Life isn't all rainbows and sunshine
But Life also isn't all doom and gloom
Life is the yin and yang
It is a delicate dance between the two

I choose to embrace it all
Not just what's impressing
For the darkness has lessons
And the light has blessings

Without one or the other
Life loses its purpose
I'm not trying to be all positive or all negative
I'm just trying to be authentic

And sometimes with authenticity comes uncomfortability
Because in calling myself out You will see too
Sometimes we must look within
To find our own truth

It takes a lot of work
With healing as the goal
But along the journey
We find our soul is made whole

With golden love we mend
The broken pieces that once were
By loving ourselves first
We embrace love and defeat hurt

And so, no, I'm not sorry
For this beautiful masterpiece
I am grateful for the experience
Of learning what it means to be me

~ A. Rae

Sleeping Volcanoes

In southeast Missouri, there are sleeping volcanos,
        true mountains birthed when magna cleaved
        the mantle and expelled the afterbirth of ash,

lava, and gas. The state owns those mountains now.
        Along with a handful of corporations
        of modern alchemy smelting lead to gold.

Families with babies, friends with beers, lovers
        hand-in-hand, schoolchildren in single file,
        hike across the dome, hardened over time.

None of them contemplate, even acknowledge,
        the fire beneath their soles. This fire, too, sleeps,
        a Behemoth, bent on one day remerging

from an eon of hibernation. If from ash we came,
        then, perhaps, we will return to fine tephra.
        Like falling angels, we will pall the earth.

I often wonder what is hidden beneath our annealed skins,
        our cloaks, masks, cosmetics, personae?
        When we smooth our fingertips across

another's nose, mouth, forehead, lips, is this not
        topography formed by violence, stress,
        fault, fissure, this landscape we name our face?

~ Richard Stimac

Borrowed Blood

Haibun

The artist wandered the Polish wilderness. His art was born from borrowed blood. He followed hunters, men who saw him as an oddity, a specter haunting their trails. In the crisp air of the Eastern Carpathians, he traced the paths of their kills, the blood of deer, boar, and sometimes wolves, guiding him to his canvases. Today, he trailed a pair of hunters, their rough laughter carried on the wind. He moved silently, eyes sharp, until he found the fresh blood trail of their latest quarry. He crouched beside it, dipping his brush into the crimson smears. His canvas, a piece of white linen stretched over a frame, leaned against a tree. With deliberate strokes, the artist painted the scene of the hunt—The blood added a raw, visceral quality to his work, a macabre beauty that ink or paint could never capture. His hands moved with an urgency, a reverence, as if each stroke was a prayer. The forest was his cathedral, and the blood, immortalized in shades of red and brown, was his faith. Completed—he leaves the canvas at the base of the of the tree. The hunters would find it come morning, as they always did, and wonder at the ghost who followed them. They never knew his name.

Murders of crows watch
Satisfied with the outcome

~ Rick Christiansen

They Came by Day

It began behind the kitchen sink, a steady sequence of ants
maneuvering around the mismatched coffee mugs,
over the pickup sticks of cutlery, scavenging the plates
for crumbs & bits of breakfast. Day they came & night
they came, sent into this war zone with the order:
"Find the almond butter & transport the lot back
to barracks. Fend off intruders or carry them
to me. There will be a reckoning before the feast."

I stood over it all looking upon these creatures as God—
God of mercy & benevolence (as mankind has deliberated
it, & written it in their Good Book)—& saw the ants
prospering, the spoils of breakfast carried off
in their teeth, watched a brown recluse bolt from beneath
the crumplings of a grease-streaked napkin,
scuttling for its place of darkness to see things
unfold with its eight watchful eyes, as the ants
kept to their lines in a never-ending loop across the counter
like a neon sign—making their way, then slipping back
out of sight through the seam where wall meets counter
to reassemble before the C.O. of ants.

But day they came. And night they came, fending &
    foraging.
And then—I admit— as a vengeful God, I showed my
    temper
& smote much of this dogged wave, snapping
a neatly striped towel across their backs, their remains
mottling the cotton. I said a quick prayer,
grabbed the sprayer & sent the rain in floods
to sweep away the rest—down, down, down

the drain--mission aborted. The few survivors, breaking
ranks, made their frenzied way out of my line of sight.
But day they came & night they came.

So, I laid down my plan, as a daring God, folding a sheet
of paper towel, creating, in one minute, a mountain
of almond butter & covered it in sweet, sweet Liquid Terro©
to embolden them & set it out on the counter.
I would provide a rapture like no other.
And then I rested.

And day they came & night they came, black streams
spilling out of the chasm, making their way
around the faucets, over the bowls, persisting
over the pans, oblivious to every obstacle
in their march to the summit.

And there they danced & sang,
crawling for joy in the glory of it.
And most carried away what they could,
& some got a little drunk, & some
were booby-trapped in the tarry butter itself.
And soon there were few.

In my final act, as a calculating God,
I measured, end-to-end, the fissure
where they fell back to base,
& ran a bead of caulk along it
until I was satisfied
their winter would come, cold & brutal.
My will be done.

Then I washed the dishes.

~ Cortney Daniels

Up on the Inishowen

Cionn Mhálann- "Malin Head" is the most northerly point of mainland Ireland, at the very end of the Inishowen Peninsula in County Donegal. The head's northernmost point. called Dunalderagh, lies at latitude 55.38°N It was the last of Ireland to be seen by the intrepid followers of St. Brendan, who sailed across the North Atlantic in the late 5th and 6th Centuries to spread the gospel.

Ptolemy knew of this cold grey place;
Boreion on his map, the last of the north,
the end of the knowable world, the wilderness
where edged rocks like teeth gnashed
the Atlantic into bits of splash
and spray.

Stouthearted monks departed this headland
where grasses grasp for life, in skin boats,
their faith rowed north to icy-watered know-not-where,
armed with Brendan's prayers, by stars to the Stones of
Faroe, on to Iceland, shores whom only God had known
were yonder.

Imagine their joy at the sight of land! After many stormy
weeks tossed about like a leaf in the wind, with brothers
lost at sea, having to drink sheep's' blood once freshwater
was gone, eating raw mutton strips, all of the corporeal
sacrifices to get here and then—their great grievous
disappointment—God had delivered them unto shores,
where they would die,
where there were no souls
to be saved,
but their own.

I stood, stared out across that dark iron grey sea, beneath churning, wind ripped skies. What would I have believed if this was the end of my only world? Would my faith deliver me to lands of demonic monsters and devils, into the hands of unlearned heathens that might lurk beyond these tides– or in my mind –that Christ could have sent me forth

to slay or save?

~ Jude MacAllen-Tatman

Christ-like

I am, unashamedly, a follower
Of Jesus Christ, who taught
Us by stating, "Love
One another, as I have loved you."

However, I hear those who call
Themselves Christians as they belittle
And degrade ones not like them.

Perhaps someone should remind
Them that Jesus did not say,
Love one another, except for
Those gay boys standing down
On the corner together, and
Those who don't look like you,
And those who do not believe
As you believe.

His message was very simple ...
Love.

~ m. pottorff

Country Roads

perfect families
dinners on tables
"bless us oh, Lord"
we walk
share our common stories
we do not want to go home

home
where they take without concern
use their child's body
objectify defile
even her younger sister, she said
was not to be spared

when the car pulls up
driver asking directions
we see it naked in his hand
and do what we cannot do
at home
we turn and run

run for the trees
silent   safe
how does it feel to be safe
at home in your bed?

I hear she got caught up
with a rough crowd
too many drugs

killed herself they shrug and say
just another crazy girl
gone astray

~ Sharon SingingMoon Feltman

An All-Nighter on the Turnpike

Through Pennsylvania, the hills break the sky up
into smaller skies, into endless blue profiles.

Across their land, animals move alone: badgers & deer,
'possums & dogs. We're moving with them as the sky

reorganizes & raptors wheel over the roadside
where the dead are collecting, eyes open.

They capture the moon's honed light
& glow like moonstones. Nothing moves them.

We pass into dawn, & those stares seem defiant
as if the sky, reflective, would turn these deaths

to its advantage, but nothing moves this stillness.
Nothing gets in the way of the ongoing process

of decay. The hawks are circling their mark.
The ravens & vultures alight to feed—

piercing the eyes, thinning those abandoned houses
of fur—then thrust skyward with their offerings.

A summer's drive through Pennsylvania.
Heat shimmers trick our eyes. The air stops moving.

Somewhere we can't see, a nest is forming
around a scavenger's eggs. Along roadsides,

the soft parts, the remainders, are melting away—
unlike the bones that hold up road-hard. We see

them glow like lovely moonstones across shoulders.
We look now because the slipstream of traffic

will push them, finally, into their ditch graveyards.
Families will stop looking for them. The dead

are melting away. Through Pennsylvania,
the hills break the sky up into smaller skies.

~ Cortney Daniels

Collateral Damage

Viktoriia's sign,
"Children are not Nazis!"

My sign promotes compassion, kindness,
unity. With hearts dressed in colors for Ukraine.

The protest on a busy corner daily at 5:00pm.
Viktoriia's baby naps in a carrier

against a warm bosom
as Putin bombs schools

and soldiers massacre mothers
with newborns.

Honking cars respond with loud wails.
People pull over to get free signs.

STOP RUSSIA!
SAVE LIVES IN UKRAINE!

Viktoriia calls her family there daily.
Another Ukrainian friend

hasn't heard from her relatives
for weeks now. "We're hoping

it's just that
the internet is down."

But in Mariupol -
mass graves.

Another friend's elderly father
who has Parkinson's

is nearly abandoned
as helpers have fled.

She's on the phone daily
pleading for others

to aid this man in his nineties.
Get him his meds. Some food.

Across the street from our crowd in blue and yellow
stands a bearded man as old as war,

holding his hunched-over sign, "Save Palestine."
I can see through him

to his dissolving joints. We wave.
He teeters off, still seeking recovery.

~ Barbara Leonhard

Go Vote

For the love,
of all that you hold dear.
For the fear,
of all that terrifies you.
Go vote.

Go vote, because you must.
Go vote because you should.
Go vote, for the ones who died
to give you this gift.

Go vote for your daughter,
for your sisters and lovers.

Remember dear children,
we do not want
to take our country back.
It is our job,
to take the country FORWARD.

~ Caitlin Korte

California Sketches 4x4

Anaheim 1955

The structures rise up out of the plundered orange groves.
An edifice of imagination tempered by hope and greed.
Already lesser persons take a stand.
Filling the easement with fading opportunities.

Santa Monica 1967

The sand is firmly packed by drug addled heels.
Pounding like the surf to a Motown beat.
God has a work order in place.
The craftsmen are eager to begin.

East LA 1979

The donut shop sells malt liquor now.
A small Vietnamese woman gives change scornfully.
Dropped candy melts in pools by the curb.
It hasn't rained in a long time.

LA Streets 1991

High speed intoxication spawns police retaliation.
Rodney King is beaten beyond recognition.
89 seconds captured which makes the news.
Justice twinkles briefly, but then is lost.

~ Rick Christiansen

Corona Migrainosus

Cosmic slow slide
flares anticipation.
Dusky darkening.
See there's Venus, maybe Mars!

Drinks and jokes abound.
A transcontinental swath
of recently crowned
babes get swaddled

before being christened
Luna Sola Corona,
Bailey Diamond or
Besselian Umbra Saros.

But here on the patio
blood rushes my ears.
Hums like angry bees.
Wavers. Surges. Horizon
throbs. Unyielding nausea
overshadows me.

Vertigo doesn't know how to count,
can't manage to keep time,
nor inhibit its impulse for total obliteration.

Furious migraine rages eight days beyond totality.
In 2024, will I have the self-control
to join the Navajo who look away?

~ Cam Whelr MD

Picasso Dreams Broken Glass

-In response to the insurrection at the U.S. Capitol (2021) -

Thrust down with a fumbling hand
in the light of the slumberous moon
crashing into the crater in my chest
all that pain of after death, the broken glass,

the splintering cries of those who gather by the gate
& wonder where to go & who to see
& ask if there's a place for their guns
or something organic to eat,

but why cast onto me
this surreal art of disharmony:
jumbling discordant shards,
the jagged insurrections of clouds
& murders by crowds,

& those who rage, their fire snuffed out
by wet whimpers
& so they drown in grief,
but why pursue me, as though I

could decode this absurd collage,
takc on the lake effect breeze
of a dense fog that steeps
in a mind that cannot sleep,

much less dream of rainbowed gardens.
Why seek me to recast their shattered sorrow,
scattered chaotic clutter,
their Felliniesque costumes?

I don't know the half of it.

~ Barbara Leonhard

Civic Lesson

I live in a foreign land
backwater   barbaric
where the death penalty is
accepted   condoned   imposed
without a second thought

ask Marcellus Williams
convicted   sentenced
in 2004   on death row
the only evidence –
two informants

one a former girlfriend facing
solicitation charges, the other
a fellow prisoner, suspended
sentence, and both paid cash
what could go wrong there?

until 2017, when the governor
formed a board of inquiry
to evaluate a clemency request
new evidence, DNA
that demonstrates his innocence

evidence still not heard in court
is meaningless when
an inquiry issued by a governor
can be dissolved by a governor
with no avenue for appeal

the governor, successor to
the previous, dissolved the board
without hearing its recommendation
removed the stay of execution
now set for September

I've been in Missouri
more than ten years
my civic lesson
continues, and this seems
less like home than it ever has

~ Ken Gierke

ABC and D is for Doubt

As I delve into my history, searching for the story needed
before I can start to write, I am forced to
consider the validity of my point of view. And I doubt.

Doubt is a powerful concept.
Emotion…doubt is actually an emotion.
Feeling? Emotion? I am

getting tangled in semantics.
How do I step out of myself and
into myself at the same time without

jacking up the whole process of reflection?
Keeping this structure moving forward
looks easier than it is proving to be for

me—I have no subject—just doubt.
No point from the compass to put my finger
on to lay claim to that elusive point of view.

Proving that I have something worth saying
quickly seems futile.
Reclaiming my place to write is

something that I try to do daily.
The process of finding anything that promotes
understanding or creates real connection or

value to those around me or anyone in the
world feels impossible in these moments.
Xenomorphic sentence structures distance me from

your perspective. I want to have certainty,
zealousness, I want to be more than a puff of smoke.

~ Rick Christiansen

TIRED

I'm tired.

Tired of people who only want sound bites.

Tired of people who are too lazy to think about nuanced points of view.

Tired of people who have never been South of St Louis whining about their Southern Heritage.

I'm tired.

Tired of people who think all police are bad.

Tired of people who think all police are good.

Tired of people who say they are not racist but say racist things.

I'm tired.

Tired of people who think that flying a traitor's flag is the equivalent of wearing trousers too low.

Tired of people who shoot their mouths off on Facebook but want to stifle criticism.

Tired of people who are against choice but for stopping SNAP.

I'm tired.

Tired of old people who are for health care for themselves but not those under 65.

Tired of people who say they are for freedom but ok with brown kids in cages.

Tired of people who claim to support the Constitution but only when they like the result.

I'm tired.

Tired of Senators who say they are for due process but refuse to allow witnesses at a trial.

Tired of politicians lying e v e r y damn day.

Tired of public corruption.

I am tired.

Tired of Baptists hating Muslims.

Tired of Muslims hating Jews.

Tired of Jews hating Catholics

I'm tired.

Tired of Democratic tribe members.

Tired of Republican tribe members.

Tired of cheap, lazy Independents who never contribute to or work for anything.

I'm tired.

Tired of thieves who cheat on their taxes.

Tired of people who who think not being inconvenienced is a Constitutional right.

Tired of people who say the minimum wage is not too low.

I'm tired.

Tired of poor people blaming other poor people for being poor.

Tired of ignorance being a virtue.

Tired of men being mean to cover for insecurity caused by low IQs and small penises.

I'm tired.

Tired of people who would sacrifice others for the economy but not themselves.

Tired of lazy, low IQ assholes who only repost memes
   because they are too intellectually challenged to have
   an original thought.
DAMN! I am just tired!

   ~ John Clayton

Too Old to Fight

Maiden, mother, crone.
Trapped in a cycle as old as time.
Breaths weaving tapestries of conflict and joy.
Of struggle and ease.
Too young to know,
Too busy to notice,
Too old to fight.

~ T.K. Pierce

Less

The words
useless
and worthless
are tricky, and kind of
misnomers.

Useless, implies that
at one point or another
I had a use.
Worthless, implies
I had a worth.

But it's so much more.
It's not just that the
use and worthiness are
gone.
No, no.
They have been
degraded,
withered away
to nothing ness.
That's all I am now
... less.

~ Caitlin Korte

The Lies I Tell Myself

The imposter in my head is writing a poem,
Is reading a poem,
Is sitting at an event giving opinions to people I respect
    like I know anything.
The imposter goes to work and answers every question
    with the utmost confidence.
She calmly solves problem after problem, before I break
    down in the car for the child I wasn't able to help.
I sit and I stew,
Watching the imposter convince the people around me
    that I know what is going on.
She isn't infallible.
The imposter still drops balls flying by my head when too
    many balls are in the air.
Her tone too sharp, cutting people while she tries for genial.
She reads a poem,
Writes a poem.
Tells people she respects opinions that feel like nothing
    to me.
Ideas prick my brain,
looking for the door out.
But the imposter is there to help me.
Telling me how my thoughts will sound better in another
    voice.

~ T.K. Pierce

Grief Magnified

Grief held me for years.
Not as captive, but it's leash
would pull when least expected.
Thoughts of your past, ours,
fond memories that could bite
as well as bring a smile.

Her sorrow for your absence,
evident at first, seemed masked
as time went on. Then,
she was gone, fifteen years
without you more than
she could bear.

Just like that, my grief,
though renewed,
was as nothing,
the weight of her own
far greater than any
I could imagine.

~ Ken Gierke

Any Thing

I can't fix anything
I can't help anything
I can't DO
any thing.

I'm here.
I take up space
and energy
and effort
and time.

But I promise
I am cheering you on.
Because well,
I can't
fucking do
any thing else.

~ Caitlin Korte

Waiting: Haibun

Out to the beach. I savor the stillness of inky darkness. Damp sand. Bare feet. The lone surf-fisher wondering the tide's edge. I turn down beach. Don't dare break this silence even with a nod. Salted-breezes shiver across my bare arms making me wish for a sweatshirt. Distant thunderheads surf the horizon. Shades only just unmasked. Last morning star pierces the moonless sky. Or maybe Venus. Gunmetal hues play tag and tumble on lapping waves. Suckle sand from beneath my toes. Turn to quicksilver. Recede. *If I stay here, I will sink. An abandoned hull.* A pair of sandpipers arrive. Dodge sea foam. Bow and dance to the song of new day's rising. I hug myself. Hurry urges me. I know this blessed peace will soon shatter into a million shards. But for now, blushing dawn whispers, *Stay. Remember. Wait. Cling to this solace.* Behind shuttered lids, I sense the growing light. The first gull's keen ruptures against the shushing wind. Internal resignation nods to the shrill signal knowing the onslaught of sun-starved masses will sweep in.

We wait here groaning.

Marooned wreckage, our longing.

Tireless tide rolls on.

~ Cam Whelr MD

Annie 2022

The whimper is like releasing steam
from a boiler. Incremental pressure
dropping, joints relax as they flex.

Pain too big to feel all at once,
needs too large to capture
in the boundaries of a moment:

desire an irritation—an itch.
She spasmodically plucks at the loose
skin on the back of her hand.

Feels the weight of the blankets,
toes tented at the foot of the bed.
He watches her stare at the button

on the morphine pump.
Sees her calculating her equation,
trying to reconcile relief with lucidity.

~ Rick Christiansen

Block 11

The fox senses what's coming
before the chase; the fly feels
the whoosh of the swatter.
I smell her before she circles.
I learn to still time like water

as the glass slips & shatters, I turn
away & purse my lips as the water drips.
I run where the soft place waits--
bury my living self inside the womb
of bed sheets before she meets me—
a hand, knuckles hard as a turtle's shell.

I've watched this mother. A fine sharp needle
she will pinch softly—such care to mend
cloth. And with those hands to smooth
its creases like a caress for a sad child.
But for this shattered glass, I hardly breathe.
Her hands show me where my soft spots live.

I wait her out & then she turns away—hear
the wood groan under her leaving feet.
The door slam rings & the lock click pings
its faraway bell sound in my ear.
The echo carries me when she's gone.
I learn to still time, wear down these long

breaths until they're hardly drawn—smell salt
& snot, streaming off cheekbones down

to the floor where my prayer rug waits—
my mermaid of perfect braids, pinks & mauves
in my ocean mirror still as time
where I learn to say a head-prayer

to God in the sky—a bed-prayer:
"Please make me good," then open
my eyes & see bears tumbling
on their giant paws & rabbits hopping
in long grass, living on the papered walls.
I've learned to still time until the breath crawls.

She leaves in one dress; the hours go circling.
Returns in another & asks, "What's hurting?"
My mother. My mother hands me
a glass with water—my narcotic.
I learn to still time like a hypnotic.
She is my cuckoo circling my hours.

I will be good, & better, & still
like water. I learn what it is
to be mother & daughter.

~ Cortney Daniels

The Solace of Seasons

I

As Spring winds blow by,
Gentle fingers tickle sky
And trees gently dance.

II

Summer night, black ... cool,
Wraps itself like thin fingers
Around tops of trees.

III

Fall whistles through trees
As moon suspends in background.
Fingers wave slowly.

IV

Winter covers trees
As frail fingers reach to God,
Seeking solace there.

~ m. pottorff

Calliope's Revenge

Calliope springs from the soil.
Her golden crown blinds the sun
with jewels, the light of violets.
She eats my cantaloupe,
sips corona, tweets with magpies.
Sad poets resting in torpor
complain she talks too much.

Homer collects her rambling texts
onto toilet paper rolls to study during Lockdown.
Submits her endless rants to Rattle
under his name, claims
AI did it. 5G made him dizzy.
The magpies out him. PEN pulls
his award, cancels the check.

Calliope's unrattled. Has new side hustles—
Metaphors Galore on Etsy and
music lessons on YouTube.
Virgil arrives in his Uber to shuffle her
to poetry readings and book launches.
Got any good lines? He asks.
She opens her purse and

fans out words like a fistful of twenties.
"All men owe honor to the poets –
honor and awe; for they are dearest

to the Muse who puts upon their lips
the ways of life." He caught it all
on his voice recorder and sped off
to write his epic.

~ Barbara Leonhard

A Lesson at the U-Pick

1.   APPLE PICKING

They stand, tree after tree, so still
I hear them breathe. Their long arms
stretch for each other, never touching.
I kick the roots--gnarly things, knit
together for miles under the hardpack
human feet have made. I reach

deep inside her canopy where twisting arms
embrace themselves, screened
in a breadth of her leaves. She has opened
her hands to show us her fruit—

such a richness of choice! Eye
witness to life, I tug a little,
transfer this one to my hand—stark
& freckled—my new red heart.

2.   WHAT SHE TOLD ME

We stand, tree after tree.
We take care of ourselves
in this orchard, where bees bow
to the king blooms, leaving their gifts
in spring & the pomes begin to form.

When cloud eclipses cross over us,
& the shadow blackens, the summer

rains begin. The wet seeps down
through the pores of our bark.
When the winds come, we dance.

When we shake ourselves small faces
fall—early & incomplete. I hear them
drop to the floor. I witness
a slow splitting of their skin
as birds feed on them & carry off the seed.

The cores gather near our roots,
wedged in the crooks of our root mounds—
black knots. We count our losses,
but we keep on bearing.

Before the gold fall leaves your prize—
your pick, whole & ready for your basket,
we are already saying goodbye.
Every tug is a year of wounds.

We will hide our bare arms under
winter snow. We will hide ourselves
in the landscape.

~ Cortney Daniels

The Valley of Death

He runs through the valley of death.
A black horse with no rider.
Alone, he runs with no fear.
Fire can't burn that which is not there.
Death cannot touch that which never lived.

~ T.K. Pierce

The Battle of C-PTSD

The demon came to battle again.
The goddess thought the war was done
So this time she wasn't prepared
For she thought her love and light had won

But the demon was tricky
For last he cast his little spell
And her mind ran rapid
Her thoughts became her hell

The goddess lived in paradise
Perfectly happy and content
This is when the demon's spell hit hard
To a hell in her mind our goddess was sent

She struggled as she tried
To handle it all on her own
Eventually her own mind convinced her
She deserved no one and she just needed to be done

She began to think how the world would be better off
If she was dead and gone
So the goddess knew she had to reach out
She needed an army to fight this one

She called in her Generals
Her closest of allies
She shared with them her perspective
And instantly they identified

They identified the spell
They helped her identify the lies
And reminded her of her worth
She promised not to follow through with her demise

She needed to make some changes
For her bliss had caught her guard down
She needed to Armour up
For the Battle was coming now

The demon had been revealed
And the goddess was prepared
She had her army and her memory
Of just who the fuck she is.

~ Ashley Rae

She Lights the Match,
We Burn the Rivers: A Cento

Angels with dirty faces
praise all the old knives,
praise all the light we cannot see,

the weight of shadows where water
comes together with other water,
wicked river,

America's original sin .
We are all suspects now.

Blood in the fruit—
the gifts of the body.
Blood of the air—
her smoke rises up forever.

Maps and mapmakers
hope in the dark.
Transformations of the lover
stop-time red

wood and wildfire. A bound
woman is a dangerous thing—
trouble behind glass doors.

Fugitive spring? We say no.
Killing floor? We say no.
The end of vandalism? We say no.

Oblique prayers—ways of seeing
strangers in their own land.

Time. And robbery.
Journey into the whirlwind—
The leopard's mouth is dry and cold inside.

~ Lynne Jensen Lampe

*Body of poem comprises titles of books by these authors in this order:
Walidah Imarisha, Robert Hass, Olin Steinhauer, Robert Hass, Anthony Doerr,
José Orduña, Raymond Carver, Lee Sandlin, Jim Wallis, Tram Nguyen, Alice
Walker, L. Timmel Duchamp, Rebecca Brown, Ama Codjoe, James Tiptree,
Jr, Allison Coffelt, Rebecca Solnit, Adonis, Frank Conroy, Andrea Hairston,
Damaris Hill, Walter Bargen, Deborah Digges, Eduardo Galeano, Ai, Eduardo
Galeano, Tom Drury, Eduardo Galeano, Denise Levertov, John Berger, Arlie
Russell Hochschild, Rebecca Orr, Evgenia Ginzburg, Marcia Southwick / Larry
Levis*

Fresh Eel

You are fresh eel
Cut into luxurious silken strips
I am sticky rice
Resting in small clumps

Both on the plate
Still separate
An expanse of porcelain
Between us

~ Rick Christiansen

Rise

With the grace
of a fat beaver or snapping turtle
that sluggishly crawls out
of the river to sun upon a mudbank;

I rise,
into this day of black coffee,
Jimmy Buffet ballads, curmudgeonly cats
and noblest dogs who warm this house
in ways only good gods could grant.

~ Jude MacAllan-Tatman

I Own My Rising

Ordinary, mostly unnoticed, I am however a woman of strong appetites, driven by patterns set in childhood, like a trail through deepest wood, tread upon step by step, worn down to bedrock. I found myself in a place, a time that, like so many places and times, valued women made of clay thrown on the wheels of men, shaped as willed by others. Even so, coming to know myself as more than a vessel holding the fantasies of others, I broke free, formed, re-formed my own destiny with tools I found along the trail and those things I could steal.

~ Sharon SingingMoon Feltman

I Need a Wrist Strap for my Ice Axe

Wearing a short dress and sandals,
I step into the outfitter, ice axe
in hand, and ask for a wrist strap.
The questions begin immediately:

What do you want with an ice axe?
Don't you know that is a dangerous
mountain? A real climb? Wouldn't you rather
be interested in a nice walk?

My bearded friends
on the other side of the store
watch for a while, amused,
before they amble over to me.

Suddenly, the wrist strap
is no problem at all.

~ Agnes Vojta

A Skiff of Snow

a skiff of snow was blowing
over the blacktop
upon bitter gusts from across the plains;
pulled my collar against the chill,
turned the other cheek—
knew she wasn't coming home, again.

the roaring of the whiskey still echoed
thru the hall; apologies lay fallow on the floor.
yesterday's coffee -like yesterday's words-
brewed bitter cold and strong; i stood
drinking the hard truth
staring out an open door.

starkness in the rooms mirrored that within
the heart, anger's plowed furrows of hate
have born indifference– a harvest of lies
brought forth steel disdain, cold as the breath
on the north wind—
it was time to pull the last string.

it fell apart in a moment yet lingered thru the night
before the shadows of a snowy dawn where it just drifted
away
into tumbling skies like a pallid wash
over fallow frigid fields.

the dead elm along the road stood sentinel
to the end of our song.

~ Jude MacAllen-Tatman

Cruel: Haibun

I went out of my way for you. You didn't notice or care. I made it easy for you. I cooked. I shopped. I baked. I cleaned. I offered. I met you. I drove you. I came your way. I went out of mine. You received and received and received. When I left, you acted shocked and wanted to know why I would do something so cruel.

Seeking friends. She stood
In the snow. Holding tickets
To a sold-out show.

~ Cam Whelr MD

Ladybug

"*Ladybug, ladybug, fly away home.*
Your house is on fire and your children are gone."

—English nursery rhyme

He didn't know what alcohol was,
except that it smelled sharp.

Like the smell when
they gave him shots at the doctor.

She mixed it with lemonade when she was alone,
on hot afternoons, with only him for company.

She called him her best buddy.
Hugged him close,
then pushed him away.

Blew cigarette smoke into his eyes
until they burned and he could not catch his breath.

When she wasn't sad or mad or drinking or crying,
they made jigsaw puzzles together.

She would remind him to find
all of the pieces with straight edges.

They would build the border,
fill it with all of the other pieces,
sorted by color and subject.

Part of a fence/
red like the bricks/
blue from the sky.

She was drinking this afternoon
and sent him outside with a grape popsicle.

She was tired of his questions.
Crying, because she had slapped him.

The sun was too warm on his face
as he sat in the dirt of the weed filled yard.

The popsicle was gone now.
He was getting thirsty.

A lady bug landed on the back
of his hand.

Sitting very still,
`hoping she would not fly away,
he wanted to be her friend.

If he became very small or
she became very large,
they would fly away together.

They would make a new home for just the two of them.
It wasn't sad there.
It was quiet and calm.

They could go over the high fence,
Away from this dry choked place.
He would not be lonely.

But now the ladybug seemed restless
and her wings fluttered.
He knew she was going to fly away.

He sat on the packed soil,
thirsty and afraid to go in.

His mother would yell.
Hold him down with her knees,
kneeling on his arms.

Tell him that it was all *because* of him.
That she too was lonely and trapped.

And, they were out of grape popsicles.

~ Rick Christiansen

Getaway Car

He was my getaway car, so I thought
Escaping towards something always
What I thought would be a safe haven ended up shattering
    me to my core

Our feet on the gas, passion tricking me to believe it'd last
He was a sleek attractive sports car whipping me around
    turns
First at fun, freeing exhilarating speeds
But as I whisper slow down, he speeds up, gears shift into
    violent turbulence

I blinked and somehow found myself in the back seat,
    someone new in the passenger
From the back I screamed, "What about me? I'm your wife,
    what about our life?"

Mangled, metal wreckage—of course it ended in collision
Caution tape wrapped around the scene, we assess the
    damage, and he tosses me the keys

Years later glimmering pieces of my shattered past poke
    at me occasionally as I try to fall asleep
Even on the evenings where my heart and mind are
    overflowing with joyous anticipation of an upcoming
    milestone, a milestone I once imagined sharing with
    a spouse
The shiny piece of the shattered past, it still pokes me
I ride the brief wave of grief

Both empowering and comforting to have arrived here
    alone
The rolling tears acknowledging the losses that happened
    along the winding roads
I gently lay the glimmering, shattered piece of the past
    down next to me
We'll both just be

It never occurred to me that I could be my own escape,
    my own stability, my own financial security. I was in
    search of a savior, an escape
Turns out I didn't need an escape, rather a gentle,
    sometimes trying, return to myself—a rediscovering

I didn't need an escape; I needed to slow the speed and
    trust myself
A divine stirring was a result of that violent collision

After my heart was ripped to pieces, I ripped the caution
    tape from my life and everything expanded
I let myself be touched in new unexpected ways
Like the way I ripped away from any expectations of
    what I was supposed to be
After the caution tape was gone, I felt everything
    differently, more deeply, more fully
More myself than ever before
After the caution tape was gone there was more
    permission to be
To be whatever I wanted with whoever I wanted however
    I wanted with no more need for getaway cars

~ Keely Alexander

Transformation of We

I'm still here
I've just been hiding underneath
The weight of the world got too heavy
And she didn't trust me

You see she started to doubt me
When I started to get strong
She thought the outcome would be different
And she got scared when she was wrong

She let fear sneak in
In the crevices and cracks
And she thought she had to grow up
To find what she lacked

The thing is if she'd trusted me
We would have made it in the end
She sees that now
I'm not a weakness but a friend

The thing in her magic
That sets her apart
Is no matter the terror she sees
I'm the child in her heart

The part of her that sees
The magic in the air
The beauty of dancing trees
And the joy in her flair

Yet her magic extends beyond
What she currently knows
She feels intensely because
In her emotions her power grows

The intensity of them
Is what makes her soul fly
Her dreams manifest
And it's where her peace lies

Between the turbulent storm
And the calming peace
Lies the transformation of a goddess
The transformation of we

For now she's remembering
That she has never lacked
It's time to focus on enjoying the experience
And letting go of the past

~ Ashley Rae

Anchor Point

You offered to be an anchor, as I approached uncertain seas.
Still in the midst of traversing your own,
a linking back, holding me close.

But little did I know
day after day,
one reassurance after the other.

Far more than an anchor,
you were ballast.

No longer in fixed points
We navigate, onward
together.

~ Caitlin Korte

Why do you want to be a poet?

"Why do you want to be a poet?"
As soon ask me why I want to be a woman?
Why do I want to have blue eyes?
Why do I want to breathe?
I do not WANT to be a poet.
I am a poet,
As I am a woman.
As I have blue eyes.
As I have to breathe.
Ask me instead:
What do I wish to make known?
What do I hear when I close my eyes?
What do my dreams sound like?
Because they all sound the same.
Poetry.

~ T.K. Pierce

I Find Myself in a Field of Henbit

For years, knee pain & inflammation. Inactivity.
The pandemic. The lockdown. Grocery delivery.
Rides in the car. Couldn't walk far.
Knee sleeves. Pain patches. Handrails.
Good leg up. Bad leg down. But then—
the good leg swells & cries, as well.
Sciatica stretches like a spider down my legs.
It eats my sleep. I'm caviar on old bones.
My mood lays black tar in my path.

What's happened to us? You ask.
No more hikes or bike rides?
One autumn day, you film your favorite hike
along the Missouri River
so that I can see the path
you created with a machete,
now part of the official trail.

At last, in February, respite
with physical therapy
for my knees & back.
An earlier surgery date in late May.
Laps with my walker on the driveway
made me stronger.

Today, my second 3-mile hike
with walking poles
on your favorite trail.

You clean the path before me,
kick the stones aside.

Here is where —
I found that huge wasp hive.
That poor raccoon kit froze to death last winter.
I created a new direction for the path.
That young buck made stomp holes
to protest my presence.
The tornado came through.

Watch out for the roots.
This one looks like a snake.
This invasive hops species will take over
everything & soon
the poison ivy will bloom.
Don't touch that. It's hemlock.

At the destination, California Island,
revealed by low water. The place
where you mine bags & bags
of carnelian agates, petrified wood,
fossil horse & camel teeth,
& mammoth bones. Sometimes arrowheads.

Startled geese take flight off the island,
& vultures soar. Owls hoot though it's day.
Across the river, a long train wails.

In the pink setting sun,
I stand in a lush field of purple Henbit.
I breathe in well-being. Gratitude for healing.
I am nurtured, ready to flourish.

~ Barbara Leonhard

Tornado Alley

Yet in the Book of Revelations, archangels posted
        at the imagined corners of the globe.
        They held back the four winds of the earth,

but must have abandoned this plot of flat land
        between Appalachia and the Rockies.
        Here, the winds master the beasts of the fields.

If you've seen a tornado, you can only think of a god,
        intemperate, implacable, a contradiction
        turning inwards. We live outside this violence

that bridges sky and ground, a pillar of clouds
        in the treeless Great American Desert.
        At least here, there is no forbidden fruit.

With each passing storm season, we remember
        that we are an unsettled people. Canaanite
        or Hebrew, either way, tornados flatten crops,

tear roofs from wood-frame houses, snap telephone poles,
        and, like words from a prophet, collapse the hubris
        from the lullaby that is the American Way of Life.

~ Richard Stimac

9/23/01

There's a certain solace that
Comes from riding a tractor.
You, the machine, the land,
And the Lord communing
In a manner only each could
Understand. It is during this
Time I know why a man
Could choose to work the land
For a lifetime. When I sit in
My office, with the window,
I sometimes think myself
Better off than those who
Have to work the land,
But on the seat of this old
Allis, I doubt my thinking.

~ m. pottorff

Potato

I've dabbled behind your back
in unfulfilling affairs.
I haven't quite recovered,
from a lingering flirtation with pasta;
the angel hair with clams, olive oil &
parmesan still seems wrapped around
my fork.

There were legumes and grains,
many liaisons in most exotic ways:
first the Cajun, piquant aromas, heat of the kiss,
Laissez le bon temps roulez!!
Red beans & rice! Jambalaya! Etoufee!
Sadly, I could not tolerate such fiery ways,
at least not every day.

And cumin scented Lebanese lentils
such a tasty paramour,
with saffron rice. But at such a price
for the golden spice, I could not afford
so set her aside. A bit of their jaundiced
zest yet sits on the shelf;
I think I saw it cry.

After frequent flings with frijoles, refried,
still I sneak a snack with queso,
chips, Spanish rice, salsa- divine!
It's all right down the way, so
I'd eat there every night-
despite the odious side effects'
blight.

There were trysts with healthier courtesans:
quinoa (meh), mashed cauliflower — no.
matter. how. was. horrid. I'd rather eat them whole.
Wild rice slow simmered with mushrooms
satisfied for a bit, but such a wood hippy!
Too nutty, musky to habitually
cook up with.

Alas, nothing satisfies like you,
my little earth apple;
I could eat you anyway,
skin of brown, yellow or red.
Your pale flesh awaits to sate
my wanton ways, and craves
for butter, garlic, salt, black pepper.
I'll have you boiled, mashed, roasted,
deep fried, baked, each and every way.

But I especially love you
sautéed Lyonnais, with onions,
both sliced thin, fried in butter and bacon
grease, crispy, a bit charred along the edges
though you're tender at heart;
just like Mom would fry—

even though she never called
you by that name.

~ Jude MacAllen-Tatman

Composed to Jelly Roll Morton's
"Hyena Stomp"

I met a hyena the color of dry earth he told me there
were many roads to where I wished to go it seemed
encouraging so why was he laughing why were his teeth
cutting a wide slit through his face then I saw the roads
the pock-marks the overgrowth downed electrical lines
some with no shoulders with sheer dropoffs vanishing
points of no light others crowded by roadside memorials
and wayside shrines to ancestor dreamers the general idea
of all this being you can't get there from here can't get
anywhere from anywhere but after a minute this hyena
points to another road there's a shaded canopy water
coolers all along the way the pavement looks brand new
it's very convenient I can see this is where he wants me
to go I'm not going there I say why not says the hyena
because that's where *you* want me to go I say I've always
been like that you can ask my third grade teacher Mrs.
Keune though I guess she's probably dead I say I'm only
going where I want to go what are you gonna do then
says the hyena go up one of them other roads you can't
even pass I say no I'm going to stand right here and not
go anywhere oh you're gonna stand right there and not
go anywhere he says that's right I say he starts laughing
again that's great that's too perfect he says just stay right
there I mean that is just as good

~ Justin Hamm

Scott (Mr. Peck)

As you lay dying in that bed,
I thought back to when we
Were both much younger.
You sat so proudly on the
Back of Saddle Tramp in
Your brown cowboy shirt
And straw Stetson. The smile
On your face told the world
Of your confidence.

I let my mind drift a few years
And you stood at attention with
Tears streaming down your cheeks
As the bugler played a military
Farewell to your Uncle Robert.
You stood in salute, showing
Your love and reverence for
That bigger-than-life man.

Then you were there on the banks
Of my pond as my family all
Camped over Memorial Day weekend.
I recalled the exaggerated look
On your face when Thomas
Caught that "whopper" of a
Catfish. You carried on about
That six inch fish, and Thomas'
Chest swelled with pride.
Then, in your fashion, you chose

A teaching moment for my ten
Year old son. You showed him how
To gut and skin the fish and how to
Wrap it in tin foil with
Salt, pepper, and butter and
Cook it in the campfire.
He looked like a king eating
His favorite meal, and you smiled
That shit-eating grin of yours
The whole time.

Just a decade later, the bottle
Had taken over, and you were
Different in so many ways.
However, if I came to
Visit Mitch when you were
There, you would have that same
Shit-eating grin on your face as
You said, "Well, Markle, what are
You doing out here?"

And now they will carry you to
That same hill where Robert
Rests, and I will choose to
Remember the boy on Tramp
With a shit-eating grin on his face.

~ m. pottorff

Looking Over the Missouri at Dusk

It is strange and sad to still be alive;
the eldest of a family line, but also
still a child, lost, alone, left behind,
just five years from the age which
the old man died, five years before
getting in and out of the boat
will become difficult, as well
as unwise.

Dad was a craftsman, a welder,
smoked Winstons, and then he grew ill
and never spoke of the poisons of either.
Stoic and strong, he made stability certain,
all that was needed, more than he as a child
had known, yet— at times
he wielded shouts and silences at me
like sticks over a cornered cowered dog;
delivering or withholding, they battered
all the same.

But at dusk, when the river flowed low
and the flatheads began to bite— *wait,*
set the hook— together we hauled in
big ones up over the gunwale and onto
the deck of the jon boat, both of us happy,
smiling, still, forever in black and white
memories, dark as bats chasing
elusive dust-winged moths, in and out
of sight, but always up there
on the wall.

The air is cool now, my breathing clean,
and dewy fatigue sneaks in. i whistle
the dogs in and turn away from the river's flow—
remorseless, ceaseless—and go home, *home*,
where a good part of this life might still
be wrought.

~ Jude MacAllen-Tatman

Early Spring – Circling

Called to the edge of the bluff, off path, back
turned from a wild prairie, I'm drawn forward
not by the eagle skimming the updrafts—
a broad lasso circling above its prey—
but the Missouri River below it.

How near the rim is near enough? How soft
its lip? How deep its maw? These running shoes
are useless for holding to damp grasses,
shifting earth, indifferent to a misstep.
I hear the breeze behind me chanting
through the ephemerals—trout lily &
trillium—stirring as if to call me
back. My only answer: "Wait! Not yet!"

A swollen current churns its carrion
& hastens east across the flood plain flats
gathering into it what's not held down,
& sometimes what is, to beat its gorgeous
heart against the Mississippi muscling
from the north at St. Louis, its tempo
picking up.

And, as one—partners spinning
their wild dance downstream, it sojourns among
swallow-tailed kites spinning rings above it.
Water swirling, it fans out like a dress
in a closing spin, across the Delta—
& spent, pushes to the sea, the salt air

mingling at its mouth, before it's swallowed
by the Gulf, seeding these clouds above me.
Somehow, it's all come back here, circling.

I've lost myself to the pattern of life—
& stop these thoughts nearly at the seam where
sky & bluff meet, where I would not dare dip
a toe, listening, instead, for what I'd
rather see—& crouching low, hear the sure
murmurings of the snowmelt squeezing through
the limestone face & feeding the waters
below me.

                Mothers--they accommodate
to our quickening—carry us, bear us,
shelter us alongside them. But we—we
jump path soon enough, our own animus
untamed, wakening, compelling us
downstream awhile to agitate against
time, to dance gleeful in the joyous dark,
before the surge slows & the burst recedes
somewhere in the debris of the muddy
bottom lands, where we must find our footing.
That's what comes to mind.

                    And some late spring day,
we will pivot seeking more solid ground—
find the path—& then consider what is
rooted across the way in prairie earth.

      ~ Cortney Daniels

Presque Isle Pilgrimage

Ever drawn by the rewards
offered by blue water,
to float upon its surface
or venture down below,

to walk along its banks in
sight of herons and cormorants,
to answer the call of lapping waves,
whether current-fed

by a mighty river or windswept
on pebbled shores with
the added gift of frosted glass,
would I not be compelled

to divert my course along the shore
of that Great Lake, Erie,
to take in a spit of land
that holds all of these, and more?

The trails of green that pass
sedate, hidden coves that,
in turn, lead out to Erie's harbor.
The lighthouses, vital aids

to navigation, most notably the tower
that gazes out onto the lake from
a miles-long sandy shore. The same
tower that was witness to vows

that will live forever in my heart.
I might divert my course
every time I pass between
Cleveland and Buffalo, but

it is not a diversion. It is
a destination, one I seek
willingly, so strong is the hold
it has on this heart of mine.

~ Ken Gierke

After Labor Day

The tourists have departed
with their boom boxes and coolers,
left behind beer cans,
sunscreen bottles, and silence.
The boys who stacked boats all summer
have gone back to school,
tanned, with broader shoulders,
a season closer to manhood.
The girl who sold ice cream and smiles
has gone, too, with the memory
of kissing a boy with sun-bleached hair
one evening down by the river.
The blue rafts are deflated and packed away.
A lone canoe is lying on the landing,
like an old turtle who has seen much
and knows how to survive through winter.

~ Agnes Vojta

As the Crow Flies

You were in my dream last night.
We were in a balloon...not hot air...conventional helium or
    hydrogen
 I guess....
we had tanks and ballast.
You were the navigator
and you wanted us to go straight over the mountains
instead of zigzagging around them.
I was dubious...but we followed your plan and arrived safely.
Interestingly…
I have no idea where it was that we arrived to…
just that it was beyond the mountains
and that we had made very good time.

~ Rick Christiansen

The Towboat

                    I pondered from our
bluff top upon a towboat,
cast to work below;

her knees pressed firmly to the bulkhead of a barge
as it's filled with sand dredged up from the river—
sand that had once lived in the snow melt of the Rockies,
or had settled
upon the Great Plains to be blown
down across the Dakotas and Nebraska,
or forced by a deluge
from a thunderhead over Iowa and Kansas to runoff
to the Waters of the People of Wooden Canoes,

the grains tumbling in the fluvial cacophony of Spring's
        symphony
of high waters until
low water, slack water, they settle in the channel,
and Capital Sand Company sucks them up,
deposits them in tall conical piles upon the left bank
of the river where they stand like the pyramids along the
        Nile,
until deposited into the rust-colored barges, to be pushed
        by the towboat

thru the silt laden current of this Missouri River,
the screws churning water so it spumed a creamed mud foam
in its wake as the towboat worked the barge thru a flow
just two fathoms deep, just a quarter league downstream

where swarthy deckhands in blue jeans, and grimy white
    t-shirts
under ill-fitting life vests, with cables and ratchets in
    hand wait
to build a tow

of fifteen barges full of sand for a greater boat of the
    line to push
downriver, to someplace, somewhere,
where people don't have enough sand
in their lives.

For a few moments,
watching the work– labors of men,
a pilot's deft skills–

Softly. I floated, letting the towboat carry me downstream
almost a half century;
I inhaled
the stagnant gasses released from the mud and muck
    pulled up
in the shallows by spinning blades, the screws scraping
the river bottom–
I heard
the rumble and roar of twin diesels' boom, belching up
black befouling petrol fumes that hung on the wind
like invisible gelatinous sheets
that you'd walk right through–
I felt
it stick to my skin, again, a membrane of fossil fuel,
to wear alongside the acrid odor of men who'd heavily
    sweat

and spit and swear and didn't give a good goddamn
if they'd stink, with bruised and scraped shoulders
hauling lines, cables, gear with hands of busted knuckles,
mashed thumbs, the slip of a ratchet,
cables and lines break! flies!
at supersonic speed, steel and nylon whips
to rip yer head off– only stories perhaps, yet
completely plausible
–just another thing in the back of a disquieted mind,
while blistering in the sun, slogging in rain; don't trip, fall,
over the gunwale, off the edge, or into that mire of doubt–
alone with thoughts on mornings fogged in,
no wind, no movement, only the low constant
vibration of those diesel engines through your feet,
into your legs, torso, down your arms,
up into your head
behind your eyes, just stop
fucking thinking about it–
and with the snap
of the flag on the jackstaff in my ear, the wind is up,
the fog lifts, the tow comes alive with groans and creaks
as it moves away from the bank, into the channel, back
    to your labors,
with the constant wind in your face and you try to move
    away
from it all, to hear something else—
sounds from home upon the wind that were free of the
    tow, away
from the rumble, the churn, the swoosh– always
    inescapable,
alongside monotonous hours, days, immeasurable weeks,
only six hours off watch, then six hours back on,

never enough sleep, thru long nights always
alone or awake for thirty days, until
dropped off somewhere downstream
at places you always thought you
wanted to see;
Cairo,
Baton Rouge,
Natchez, Vicksburg,
New Madrid, Arkansas City –
and it's a long road to get
back home.

I then shook
myself, returning to present predicaments, watching
the little towboat grinding her way back upstream
for another barge, and I turned away,

walked down to the pub,
back to these days, our times, more
lifesome years with you.

~ Jude MacAllen-Tatman

Tucson Sketches #2: The Comb

I found the wooden comb I won for best costume
in the Folklorico contest last year at Meet Yourself.
It slipped out from between the butt cheeks of the rear
seat of my car when I folded it forward to lay a cloth
for the garden mulch. I held it in my hand: Made in Mexico

& set it beside me in the suicide seat—
wondered if it had traveled north from Oaxaca
or Guanajuato or Jalisco in plain sight? Or did coyotes
dump it from a windowless van the way they do,
somewhere outside of Sonoyta? Such pretty paint,
such fine teeth! If, somehow, it crept soundlessly like

    a scorpion

in the noiseless dark through Organ Pipe, bumping up against
the cacti spines as it passed through the Res? Did it chance
upon the blue flags & find the jugs of water set just in sight
of the faint foot paths? I wonder if it stumbled over any
remains like the ones my friend, Mike, from Angel Valley

    F.H. would bag,

delivering them in style in his black hearse
to the county examiners for photographs & processing—
cutting away the cloth or searching the bleached bones,
picking away bits of what's been left of a life with tweezers—
cataloguing the teeth, the tats, the scars, marking each:
John Doe or Juanita Doe, UNKNOWN & Yr. Found,

before they ice them down in the morgue to live
their cold deaths, before noting each body
on the death map with those little red dots
you use to price your junk for a garage sale.
The dead rarely make it back home.

I pick up the brown comb, throw it in my purse to forget
about it & head out, when sooner than I thought,
I'm fumbling around so I can put it to good use
to freshen myself—I see the rotating beacon of a
    sheriff's 4X4
pulling behind me—& then I gather what he'll need
    before
he runs my plates: valid license (check), insurance card
    (check).

When I roll down the window, he bends toward me
—enough so the badge is in my line of sight—
& looks askance at my face, his flashlight in my eyes.
Proud, I never try to hide my identity, but smile & wait
for him to speak the words: "Let me see your papers,"

because I've been stopped for a moving violation
& have my documents in the glove box. But I know
he won't ask. They never do. It's what I get for being
the immigrant I am—not a squint or a word when I pass
him the license. A girl from Canada could do anything
here & get away with it in SB1070-land. "Move on,
    ma'am,"

is all I get—not even a warning. I roll up the window
& wait for him to pull out, then grab the comb & take

a good look at it—just a little dirtier & browner with
strands of my hair tangled up in it, & throw it
into the console box where it will live in the dark
    unnoticed

& think to myself: "Whew. Made it."

~ Cortney Daniels

Tuckedful

for Bonnie

In the leaving house,
handshold
nook(life running between)nook
like hidden prayers
tucked into crosslegs.
They are children
of denim damage,
each finger tilled
and starving to feed another.
Back to the corner,
there is nowhere furrow
to go but smile
for lovers,
for maybe steps,
forewarning cries is
and don't let the subduillusion
fool you:
nothing is louder
than coiled concern,
so she says nothing
until the whole world hears.

~ Jon Freeland

I Am Everything I Ever Loved

The words come out of my heart to the rhythms of my
favorite author.
The mantra in my head on a loop is a paraphrase of the
song starting the movie of the killers.
I take my coffee the way I learned to love at a conference
I will never see again.
I hear my mother when I clean.
My father when I work.
I learned to hug the best way from a dear friend.
I learned to really cry at a bar.
I am everything I ever loved, and I smile to realize that
nothing is ever truly gone, if you only look inside.

~ T.K. Pierce

The Poets:

Keely Alexander is a licensed psychologist, professor, and enthusiastic cat mom with a deep passion for understanding the human experience. Through writing, she explores themes of resilience, connection, and self-discovery, using poetry as a means to process, reflect, and engage with the world. Whether in the classroom, the therapy room, or on the page, she remains committed to caring and showing up for herself and others with compassion and authenticity.

Rick Christiansen is a former corporate executive, stand-up comedian, actor, stage director, editor and current workshop teacher.. His new book *'BONE FRAGMENTS'* just came out from Spartan Press in January. It can be purchased on Amazon, Barnes and Noble and hundreds of other platforms. He has been recently nominated for a Touchstone Award. He is a member of The Writer's Place and a member of The St. Louis Writers Guild. He and his wife Kim recentlyadopted a new puppy.

John A. Clayton is a long time resident of Maries County, Missouri, where he lives in the woods. He has worked as a wood cutter, logger, construction worker, lineman, soldier, school teacher, water tower painter, lawyer, judge and gardener. John has been published in *Gasconade Review, Wine Drunk Sidewalk: Ship Wrecked in Trumpland, Rye Whiskey Review* and *Reported For Duty*. He was Poet Laureate for Belle, Missouri during COVID.

M. Cortney Daniels (she/her) is an award-winning poet living in Columbia, MO. Drawing inspiration from her lived experience as an adoptee, she finds her muse in the psychological hum of human existence and its perpetual paradoxes: choice/coercion, war/peace, violence/gentleness, power/futility, nature/nurture. She received an MFA in Poetry from the Iowa Writers' Workshop, and her recent work has appeared in *Spillwords Press, MasticadoresUSA, Anti-Heroin Chic,* and *Silver Birch Press*. She is co-editor of *Well Versed*, the annual anthology of the Columbia Chapter of the Missouri Writers Guild and is currently is finishing a chapbook of poems based on the poets who first inspired her in her as a young writer.

Jon Freeland is a poet and performer who lives in Jefferson City with his wife, Joanna, and son, Alistair. He started the Gumbo Bottoms Open Mic in December 2019 with owner Steve Erangey and arts community coordinator Suzanne Luther. After having to pause the open mic in 2020 due to COVID-19, he restarted it as a monthly gathering in September 2021. It has continued ever since, beginning with a small group of dedicated poets and growing to include features from all over the country including New York, Indiana, Ohio, Kansas, Texas, and Florida thanks to strong friendships with the Osage Arts Community, Columbia Writers Guild, and poetry ambassadors in Rolla and St. Louis. It is these deep human connections, the love and respect that our regulars have for each other, and Steve's vision combined with Allen Tatman's genius that has fashioned the Gumbo Bottoms Single Pot Still Poetry Society (or GBSPSPS, if you're trying to call your cat), meeting the first Monday of the month at 7p except when holidays or special features push the date back.

Transplanted from Western New York, **Ken Gierke** has lived in Missouri since 2012. His love for nature, fostered by the Niagara River, continues in Missouri and is often featured in his poetry. His writing has appeared as two micro-chapbooks from *Origami Poems Project*, and his poetry appears in several anthologies, including *Well Versed* from the Columbia Writers Guild, *River Dog Zine* and the *Gasconade Review*. He has been featured by numerous online journals, including *Poetry Breakfast*, *Amethyst Review*, *Silver Birch Press*, and *Ekphrastic Review*. Two of his poetry collections have been published by Spartan Press – *Glass Awash* in 2022 and *Heron Spirit* in 2024. His poetry can also be found on his website, https://rivrvlogr.com/

Originally from the flatlands of central Illinois, **Justin Hamm** now lives near Twain territory in Missouri. He is the author of five books of poetry, *O Death, Drinking Guinness With the Dead: Poems 2007-2021, The Inheritance, American Ephemeral,* and *Lessons in Ruin,* and a book of photographs entitled *Midwestern.* He is also the creator of *Poet Baseball Cards* and the founding editor of the museum of americana. His poems, photographs, stories, reviews, and artwork appear widely in literary magazines.

Caitlin Korte is a nonprofit compliance officer who finds herself full of ornery thoughts, laughter, and deep love of her family and friends. Her writing is a way to channel these emotions and experiences, often exploring the complexities of daily life and human connection. This is her first publishing.

Lynne Jensen Lampe's poetry appears or is forth-coming in journals such as *Okay Donkey, Gasconade Review, The Inflectionist Review, THRUSH,* and *Journal of Compressed Creative Arts,* and anthologies in the US, UK, and Germany. Her debut collection, *Talk Smack to a Hurricane* (Ice Floe Press, 2022), a 2023 Eric Hoffer Book Award winner and finalist for the 8th Annual McMath Book Award, concerns motherhood, mental illness, and antisemitism. A Red Wheelbarrow Poetry Prize finalist, she edits academic writing, reads for *Tinderbox Poetry Journal,* and lives with her husband and two dogs in Columbia, MO. https://lynnejensenlampe.com.

Barbara Harris Leonhard's poetry is curated in various literary magazines and anthologies. She's also written a best-selling poetry collection *Three-Penny Memories: A Poetic Memoir* (Experiments in Fiction, 2022), which is about her relationship with her mother, who suffered from Alzheimer's. Barbara's poetry has received awards and honors from *Well-Versed 2021* and *Spillwords Press.* She has been nominated twice for the Pushcart Prize. Trending Poets named her Poet of the Year 2023. Some of her poems have been translated into Italian,

Albanian, and Chinese. This year, Barbara and Nolcha Fox launched a new book, *Too Much Fun to Be Legal,* with The Garden of Neuro Institute. Barbara is also the Editor for *MasticadoresUSA.* She lives in Mid-Missouri with her husband and their cat Jasper, who refuses to go on drives to count deer. You can follow her on her blog. *Extraordinary Sunshine Weaver.*

T.K. Pierce is a poet and performer from Missouri. Her emotion-centered style is characterized by its brevity and focus on making sense of the world around her. Pierce often writes in the moment, getting struck by inspiration and needing to get it out of her head and onto a page right then. She has been part of the Gumbo Bottoms Single Pot Still Poetry Society since 2022, and enjoys reading, embroidery, video games, and bad puns.

Mark Pottorff is a poet who takes deep pride in family and the impact of being an educator. He is full of stories about teaching poetry to his students, and how some of his favorite moments happened because he put himself in his students' shoes and always wrote when they were required to. Master of the elegy, Mark finds the most succinct, beautiful ways to capture those who have similarly impacted him. His collections include the pursuit of imagism and the delivery of pure gut-wrench emotion, representing the human battle between the need to express and release our tenderest moments and the societal pressure to keep it all in as we process the trauma of our lives.

A. Rae is a poet, painter, and dedicated community advocate. A survivor who channels her personal healing journey into her art, she uses poetry and visual art as tools for transformation and growth. Outside of her creative pursuits, A. Rae founded a mobile soup kitchen to support the homeless, homebound, and low-income individuals in her community. Her paintings have been in an art gallery, and now, thanks to Gumbo Bottoms Single Pot Still Poetry Society, she celebrates her debut poetry publication. A. Rae's poetry guides readers through a process of acknowledging pain, transmuting it into strength, and ultimately finding healing.

Sharon SingingMoon is a poet, award-winning visual artist and host of a monthly reading series, SPOKEN. Sharon lives in what is now mid-Missouri on the unceded ancestral lands of the Kickapoo, Shawnee, Ioway, Otoe, Delaware & Osage. Her poetry appears in journals and anthologies in the US, UK and Germany. She co-edited *Well Versed* anthology 2024 and, with Jason Ryberg, *Rough-Cut Elegies, An Anthology of Missouri Poets*. Her poem, *Overdose*, January 2, 2023 has been nominated for Best of the Net 2025 and her poem, *Not Even the Dead*, for a Pushcart Prize. Her latest collections, *The Weight of One Hummingbird Feather* (nominated for a 2025 Eric Hoffer Book Award) and *Random Seed*, can be found at independent bookshops across the mid-West as well as on Barnes & Nobel and Amazon.

Richard Stimac has published a poetry book *Bricolage* (Spartan Press), two poetry chapbooks, and one flash fiction chapbook. In his work, Richard explores time and memory through the landscape and humanscape of the St. Louis region.

Jude MacAllen-Tatman is a graduating candidate in the University of Nebraska-Omaha Writers Workshop, class of 2025, MFA Creative Writing: Poetry. He lives in Jefferson City, Missouri, where he and his wife, Marilee own and operate Paddy Malone's Irish Pub. Among his many passions in life are bird dogs, camping, strong coffee, and good whiskies.

Agnes Vojta grew up in Germany and now lives in Rolla, Missouri where she teaches physics at Missouri S&T and hikes the Ozarks. She is the author of *Porous Land, The Eden of Perhaps*, and *A Coracle for Dreams* (Spartan Press) and of a chapter in *Wild Muse: Ozarks Nature Poetry* (Cornerpost Press, 2022.) Agnes is associate editor of *Thimble Literary Magazine* and host of the Poetry at the Pub reading series in Rolla. Her poems have appeared in a variety of magazines; you can read some of them on her website agnesvojta.com.

Cam Whelr, MD is a poet, writer and visual artist. Her work has appeared in *Pleiades, The Rumpus, Inside Columbia* and *Well Versed.* Her writing explores embodiment from inside a trauma-forged nervous system. She is a former pediatrician who has been living with neurological disability for over two decades. Between juggling health issues, she writes, creates art and participates in the Res[t] istance. She currently resides in mid-Missouri where two affable service dogs allow her to share their home.

This project was made possible, in part, by generous support from the Osage Arts Community.

Osage Arts Community provides temporary time, space and support for the creation of new artistic works in a retreat format, serving creative people of all kinds — visual artists, composers, poets, fiction and nonfiction writers. Located on a 152-acre farm in an isolated rural mountainside setting in Central Missouri and bordered by ¾ of a mile of the Gasconade River, OAC provides residencies to those working alone, as well as welcoming collaborative teams, offering living space and workspace in a country environment to emerging and mid-career artists. For more information, visit us at www.osageac.org

Osage Arts Community

www.ingramcontent.com/pod-product-compliance
Lightning Source LLC
Chambersburg PA
CBHW031514120626
46545CB00005B/1868